Science Encyclopedia

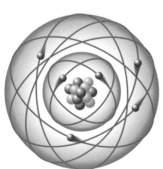

A DORLING KINDERSLEY BOOK

LONDON, NEW YORK,
MELBOURNE, MUNICH, and DELHI

Senior Editors Carrie Love, Caroline Stamps,
and Ben Morgan
Senior Designer Rachael Smith
Design team Gemma Fletcher, Hedi Gutt,
Laura Roberts-Jensen, Mary Sandberg,
and Poppy Joslin
Editorial team Lorrie Mack, Alexander Cox, Wendy
Horobin, and Joe Harris
Picture Researcher Liz Moore
Proofreader Anneka Wahlhaus

Consultants Donald R Franceschetti
and John Farndon
Packaging services supplied by White-Thomson
Publishing Ltd., Big Blue, and Bookwork

Publishing Manager Bridget Giles
Art Director Rachael Foster
Category Publisher Mary Ling
Production Editor Clare Mclean
Production Controller Pip Tinsley
Jacket Designer Natalie Godwin
Jacket Editor Mariza O'Keeffe

First published in Great Britain in 2009 by
Dorling Kindersley Limited,
80 Strand, London, WC2R 0RL

ISBN 978-1-40533-711-3
Colour reproduction by MDP, UK
Printed and bound by Toppan, China

Discover more at
www.dk.com

Contents

What is science?

Life science

There is a question at the bottom of each page...

About this book

The pages of this book have special features that will show you how to get your hands on as much information as possible! Look out for these:

The **Curiosity quiz** will get you searching through each section for the answers.

Become an expert tells you where to look for more information on a subject.

Every page is colour-coded to show you which section it is in.

weird or what? These buttons give extra weird and wonderful facts.

What is science?

Science is the search for truth and knowledge. It holds the key to understanding life, the Universe … and almost everything! To make it easier to study, scientists divide science into different areas.

From atoms to space

Scientists study a huge variety of things, from the tiniest atoms that make up everything around us to the mysteries of space.

Everything you see is made up of microscopic atoms.

Life science

How do living things survive and grow, where do they live, what do they eat, and how do their bodies work? Life science seeks to answer such questions about the living world, from microscopic bacteria to plants and animals – including you!

The scientific study of plants is called botany.

Physical science

This science looks at energy and forces. There are different types of energy, including light, heat, and sound. Forces are the things that hold everything in place in our world. Without the force of gravity, for example, you would fly off into space!

We have learned to send energy to where it is needed.

Life science studies the living world around us.

Planet Earth

4

Earth and space science

Earth is a dot in a vast Universe filled with planets and moons, stars and galaxies. As far as we know, Earth is special because it is the only place that supports life. Earth and space science is the study of the structure of our planet – and everything that exists beyond it.

The scientific study of volcanoes is called volcanology

Materials science

Our Universe is filled with atoms and elements, molecules, mixtures, and compounds. Materials science is the study of these things, how they behave, how we use them, and how they react with one another.

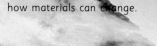

One branch of science studies how materials can change.

Pictures of Earth from space help scientists understand Earth better.

All about change

People always want to make life better, and that's what puts us on the road to scientific discovery. Whether it's inventing the wheel, or sending rockets into space, science drives us onwards, changing the world we live in.

Advances in science

Science begins with problems. The world's great scientists were all thinkers who wanted to solve life's problems. This need for understanding has produced many great inventions and discoveries.

Stories suggest Newton discovered gravity with an apple.

Newton found that white light was made up of seven colours.

Johannes Gutenberg (1400–1468)

Gutenberg played a key role in printing. Experts believe he invented metal-type printing in Europe. Gutenberg's press was quick, accurate, and hard-wearing, compared to earlier woodblock printing.

Gutenberg's first printed book was the Bible in 1455.

Isaac Newton (1642–1727)

Newton investigated forces and light. He realized there must be a force that keeps the planets in orbit around the Sun. Today we know this as gravity. Newton also discovered that white light is made up of all the colours of the rainbow.

1400   **1500**   **1600**

Wooden replica of da Vinci's Ornithopter.

Galileo Galilei (1564–1642)

Galileo proved that the Earth moves around the Sun by looking at the Solar System through a telescope. A few wise thinkers had always suspected the truth, but most people at the time believed that our Earth was the centre of everything.

Replica of a 17th-century telescope

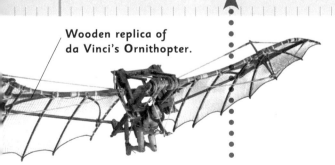

Leonardo da Vinci (1452–1519)

Da Vinci was a painter and inventor. He drew plans for helicopters, aeroplanes, and parachutes. Unfortunately, the technology of the time was not good enough to build any that worked.

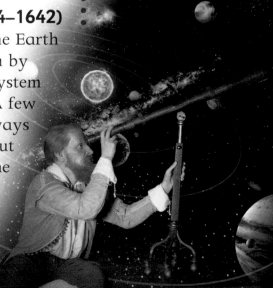

Who invented the bifocal lens?

A kite helped Benjamin Franklin learn about lightning and electricity.

Benjamin Franklin (1706–90)

American scientist Benjamin Franklin experimented with lightning and electricity. His work in the 1700s laid the foundations for today's electrical world.

Franklin risked his life flying a kite in a storm.

Louis Pasteur (1822–1895)

Best known for discovering pasteurization (a process that uses heat to destroy bacteria in food, particularly milk), Pasteur also discovered that some diseases were caused by germs. He encouraged hospitals to be very clean to stop germs spreading.

Inventions

Inventions and discoveries have changed the course of our history.

 Wheel (3,500 BCE) The first known wheel was used in Mesopotamia.

 Paper (50 BCE) This was invented in China, but kept secret for many years.

 Compass (1190) The magnetic compass was first used by the Chinese.

 Parachute (1783) The first one flew centuries after Leonardo made his drawings

 Steam train (1829) The earliest successful model reached 48 kph (30 mph).

 Colour photo (1861) First produced by physicist James Clerk Maxwell.

1700

1800

William Herschel (1738–1822)

Herschel is well known for his work in astronomy (he first identified the planet Uranus). He also discovered infrared radiation – this technology is used today for wireless communications, night vision, weather forecasting, and astronomy.

Wilhelm Conrad Röntgen (1845–1923)

Röntgen discovered electromagnetic rays (known today as x-rays) on November 8th, 1895. His important discovery earned him the first Nobel Prize in Physics in 1901.

X-rays allow doctors to look inside the human body.

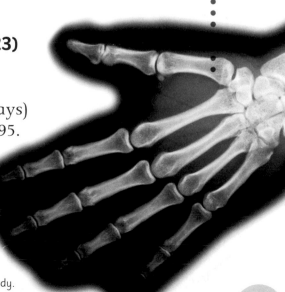

Advances in science

Movie projectors developed quickly after Edison's early work.

Early movie projector

Thomas Edison (1847–1931)
Thomas Alva Edison produced more than 1,000 inventions, including long-lasting light bulbs, batteries, and movie projectors.

Karl Landsteiner (1868–1943)
Austrian-born physiologist Landsteiner discovered that human blood can be divided into four main groups – A, B, AB, and O. This laid the foundation of modern blood groupings.

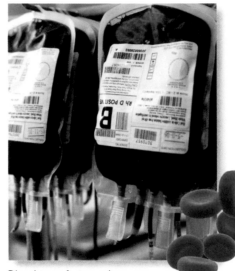

Blood transfusions play an important part in modern medicine.

Orange juice is a good source of vitamin C.

Albert Szent-Györgyi (1893–1986)
The Hungarian scientist Albert Szent-Györgyi is best known for detecting vitamin C. He also pioneered research into how muscles move and work. He won the Noble Prize for physiology and medicine in 1937.

You inherit your blood type from your parents.

Red blood cells

1800

1850

Albert Einstein (1879–1955)
German-born physicist Albert Einstein's famous equation E=mc2 explained how energy, mass, and time are all related. It helped scientists understand how the Universe works.

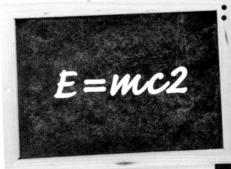

Einstein's equation

A "great" earthquake (8–9.9 on the Richter scale) strikes on average once a year.

Earthquakes destroy homes and office buildings.

Charles Richter (1900–1985)
Richter developed a way to measure the power of earthquakes. He worked on his scale with fellow physicist Beno Gutenberg.

Epicentre

Who invented frozen food?

Alan Turing (1912–1954)

During the Second World War, Alan Turing, a brilliant mathematician, helped develop code-breaking machines that eventually led to the invention of modern computers.

The English used the Enigma machine to break German codes during World War II (sometimes known as WWII).

Today's computers are lightweight and portable – early models filled whole rooms.

Modern inventions

Imagine the world without these fantastic inventions:

Antibiotics The first antibiotic, penicillin, was discovered accidentally.

Cars Some of the early models were driven by coal or wood-fired engines.

Nuclear power is efficient, but some people think it could harm us.

Plastics technology is used to make many of the things in your home.

Compact disks are small and light, and they store lots of information.

Energy-efficient light bulbs help save energy in your home.

Computers (1941)

The first computers were huge machines. They couldn't cope with complicated tasks, but worked on only one thing at a time.

Modern mobile phone

Mobile phones (1980s)

Developed from the two-way radios of the 40s and 50s, the first mobiles were large and heavy, weighing about 35 kg (77 lbs) – the same as a 10-year-old child.

900

1950

DNA discovered (1953)

The identification of DNA (which holds information in human cells) led to DNA profiling, a huge help to the police – criminals can now be identified by a single hair or spot of blood.

Nuclear bombs (1945)

Sometimes science creates monsters, like the bombs the USA dropped on Japan in WWII. They killed nearly 300,000 people and ended the war.

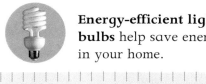

The internet (1990s)

With its roots in the 1960s, the Internet (short for International Network) became public during the mid 90s, and is now used for fun and education by about 1.5 billion people.

Before DNA profiling, police identified criminals by their fingerprints. This system was developed in the 1890s.

Being a scientist

Scientists study the world around us. They look for gaps in our knowledge and try to find the answers. Not all scientists study the same things – they specialize in different areas.

Experiments can involve toxic fumes or chemicals that might explode, so scientists wear protective goggles.

Testing, testing

Scientists explore their ideas and theories using tests called experiments. In this book, there are lots of experiments you can do to "get mucky", and try things out for yourself.

Mixing it up

Experimenting with chemicals and their reactions can produce some mixed results. Some mixtures can be dangerous, while others can be the answer the scientists are after.

How much bigger do things look through a microscope?

A closer look

Hooke's microscope

During the 17th century, the microscope was developed by Dutchman Anton van Leeuwenhoek and refined by Robert Hooke in England. Early models revealed the tiny organisms in water, while modern versions can look inside a single cell.

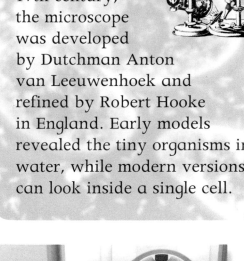

Inside view

When you go to hospital, the doctor may send you for a body scan. Using a powerful machine, the medical team can see what's going on inside you.

Get mucky

Fill a cup or vase with water, and add a few drops of food colouring. Cut the end off the stem of a flower and put the flower in the water.

Plants take up food and water from the soil and transport it up the stem. Experiments allow scientists to observe and theorize how things work and why.

Types of scientist

Almost everything in the world is the subject of study by a scientific specialist.

 Zoologists study animals of all kinds, except for human beings.

 Biologists are interested in everything about life and living organisms.

 Paleontologists know about fossils, and try to learn from them.

 Botanists learn about the world of plants, plant types, and plant groups.

 Chemists study elements and chemicals, and they help make new substances.

 Astronomers are experts on space, the planets, the stars, and the Universe.

 Entomologists are a special kind of zoologist who learn about insects.

 Geologists find out about our Earth, particularly by studying rocks.

Archaeologists are interested in the remains of past peoples and lives.

 Ecologists study the relationship between living things and their environment.

 Oceanographers know all about ocean life and landscapes.

Science and everyday life

Science is not just used by experts working in laboratories. It is part of all our lives. From brushing your teeth to setting your alarm, science is with you all day, every day.

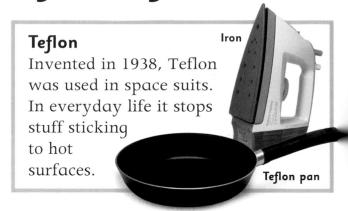

Teflon

Invented in 1938, Teflon was used in space suits. In everyday life it stops stuff sticking to hot surfaces.

Iron

Teflon pan

Electricity

Electricity lights up the world and gives us the energy to cook, travel, work, and play.

Cities at night are bright places, lit up by office, house, and street lights.

Plastic building blocks

Plastic fantastic

Look around you and you will see dozens of things made of plastic. From containers to toys, plastic is a versatile and hard-wearing material. Many plastics can now be recycled.

Plastic medicine bottles

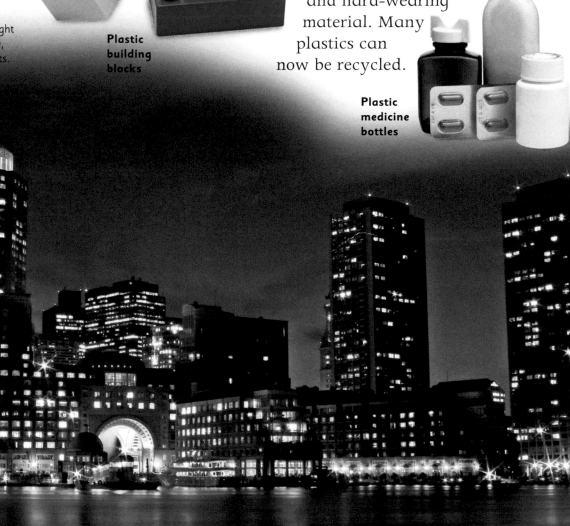

What was the first satellite in space?

Surgeons get a helping hand from computers.

Satellite orbiting the earth

In the best of health

Long ago, people relied on herbs to produce cures for disease. Thanks to modern science, many illnesses that were once untreatable can now be cured or prevented.

Masks, aprons, and gloves help doctors keep operation rooms free from infection.

Communications

Satellites orbit the Earth, beaming back all sorts of information. They send TV signals, supply weather information, and help us gaze into space.

Clothing technology

Advances in sports clothing technology have impacted on everyday clothes. Breathable fabric, stretchy spandex, and thermal underwear were developed from specialized sports and leisure clothes.

From here to there

Science and technology make it much easier to get around. Trains, planes, and cars make the world a smaller place and allow us to visit exotic destinations. They are also useful for getting to school on time.

As fast as a speeding bullet train...?

Bullet trains in Japan travel up to 300 kph (186 mph).

Become an expert...
on health, pages 40–41
on electricity, pages 76–77

Sputnik 1, it was launched by the Soviet Union in 1957.

The living world

Our amazing world is filled with millions of species, or types of living thing. They can be as big as an elephant or so small you have to look through a microscope to see them.

Spider

Dragonfly

Animals

The animal kingdom is made up of vertebrates (animals with a backbone) and invertebrates (animals without a backbone).

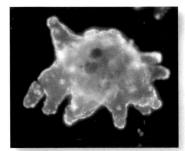

Micro-organisms

Micro-organisms are very tiny – they are made up of a single cell. This amoeba is magnified more than 100 times.

Sunflower

Mammals, birds, reptiles, amphibians, and fish are vertebrates.

Coral reef

Deer

Which group of animals has the most members?

Snake

Insects such as butterflies are invertebrates.

Plants

Plants cannot move around like animals. To survive and grow, they have to make their own food. In turn, plants provide food for many animals and fungi.

Signs of life

Living things share some characteristics. They all need food and oxygen. They also grow, reproduce, and adapt to their environment.

Fungi

Fungi (like toadstools, mushrooms, and moulds) are neither plants nor animals, but they're more like plants than animals.

Fungi

Tree frog

Curiosity quiz

Look through the life-science pages and see if you can identify the pictures below.

Become an expert...

on how plants work, pages 22–23

on types of animals, pages 28–29

Invertebrates – they make up 97 per cent of all animal species.

Micro life

Most living things are made up of just one cell, and are too small to see. To study them we must use powerful microscopes.

Bacteria

Bacteria are single-celled life forms. They are found in the ocean, in the air, and even in our bodies. They can reproduce very quickly by splitting in two. Some bacteria can make energy from sunlight. However, most feed on dead plants and animals.

Harmful bacteria

Some bacteria can cause serious illnesses such as cholera and tetanus. Good sanitation and antibiotic drugs help fight diseases caused by harmful bacteria.

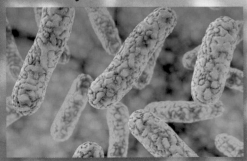

Bacteria may be shaped like rods, spirals, or spheres.

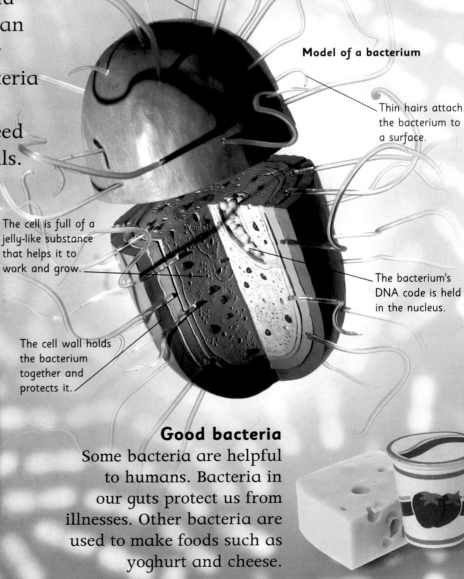

Petri dish

Each spot on this petri dish is a colony made up of thousands of bacteria.

Bacterial colonies

Whip-like structures push the bacterium along. They spin round like screws.

Model of a bacterium

Thin hairs attach the bacterium to a surface.

The cell is full of a jelly-like substance that helps it to work and grow.

The bacterium's DNA code is held in the nucleus.

The cell wall holds the bacterium together and protects it.

Good bacteria

Some bacteria are helpful to humans. Bacteria in our guts protect us from illnesses. Other bacteria are used to make foods such as yoghurt and cheese.

How many copies can a single bacterium make of itself in 24 hours?

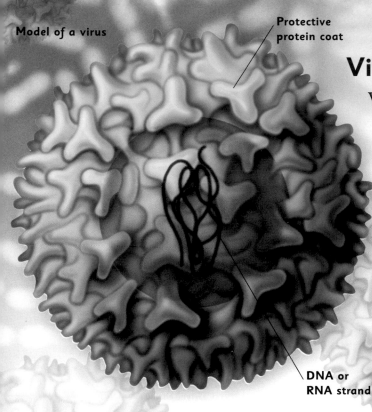

Model of a virus

Protective protein coat

DNA or RNA strand

Viruses

Viruses are many times smaller than bacteria. They are shaped like spheres or rods. Viruses are not really alive, because they are not made of cells. They only become active when they invade a cell. They copy themselves by taking over the cell and turning it into a virus factory.

Plant viruses

Plant viruses can change the way that plants develop. For example, one virus affects the pigment in tulips' petals. It stops the pigment from working in some places. This makes the petals look stripey.

A virus has made light patches appear on these leaves.

The streaked patterns on this tulip are caused by a virus.

Vaccinations

Vaccinations can help to protect people from harmful diseases. A person is injected with a weakened form of a virus or bacterium. This prepares the immune system for the real thing.

Harmful viruses

Viruses can cause different illnesses.

Chickenpox is easy to catch. The main symptom is spots that itch.

Rabies is a fatal virus that is common in animals such as dogs.

Colds are viruses and can bring on a sore throat, runny nose, and cough.

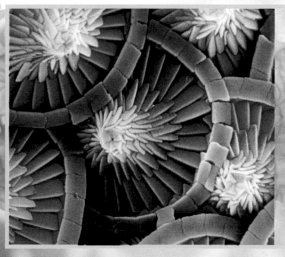

Protists

Protists are another kind of single-celled life form. They are very varied. Some protists are similar to fungi, animals, or plants. Some protists group together into colonies.

It can make 4,000 million million million copies.

Fungi

Mushrooms, toadstools, yeasts, and moulds are all kinds of fungi. Fungi are neither animals nor plants. They feed on living or dead animals or plants, and absorb their nutrients.

Bread mould

Warm, moist bread

Moulds

Moulds are microscopic fungi which grow in long strands called hyphae. They feed on dead organic matter – like our food – by making it rot.

Mushrooms

Many fungi are hidden in the soil, or inside food sources like trees. They only become visible when they grow mushrooms. Mushrooms scatter spores, which will grow into new fungi.

Gills

Stem

The gills release spores into the air.

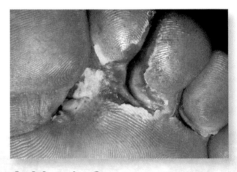

Athlete's foot

Athlete's foot is a disease caused by ringworm fungi growing on human feet. It makes the skin between your toes turn red and flaky.

Picking wild mushrooms

Many wild mushrooms are not only edible, but delicious. However, others are highly poisonous! Harmful mushrooms are often called toadstools. They sometimes use bright colours to warn animals not to eat them.

The poisonous fly agaric mushroom changes its shape as it matures. The rounded red cap flattens to reveal the gills.

Wood blewit mushroom

Penny bun mushroom

Jelly antler fungus

Where is the world's largest mushroom?

Penicillin

In 1928, Sir Alexander Fleming made an important discovery. He realised that the mould *Penicillium notatum* makes a chemical that kills bacteria. That chemical, called penicillin, is used today as a medicine to treat many illnesses.

Sir Alexander Fleming (1881–1955)

Penicillin on a petri dish

The bacteria have retreated from the penicillin, leaving a clear ring.

Truffles

Truffles are strong-smelling fungi that grow underground. They are a delicacy used in cookery. Truffle hunters use pigs and dogs to sniff them out.

White truffle

Black Perigord truffle

Yeast

Yeast are microscopic, single-celled fungi. When they feed, they turn sugar into carbon dioxide gas and alcohol. Yeast plays an important part in bread making. As it releases gas, it makes bread rise.

Uses of fungi

Fungi have many uses in the home and in industry.

 Medicine: Fungi are used in different medicines, such as antibiotics.

 Wine: Yeast turns grape juice into wine by making sugar into alcohol.

 Cheese: Blue cheeses are made with a mould called *Penicillium roquefortii*.

 Soy sauce: This is made by adding fungi and yeast to soy beans and roasted wheat.

 Pesticide: Fungi can be an environmentally friendly way of killing insects or weeds.

Shaggy parasol mushroom

Shaggy cap mushroom

Common chanterelle mushroom

Chicken of the woods fungus

Malheur National Forest, USA, it covers 8.9 square kilometres (3.4 square miles).

19

What is a plant?

Plants make their own food from the Sun's rays. Most have leaves that reach outwards to capture sunlight, and roots that dig deep for nutrients and stability.

Plant parts

There are loads of different plants. But most are made of the same vital parts – roots, stems, leaves, and flowers.

Stems

Stems support the leaves and flowers and allow water and food to flow from the roots to the leaves.

Roots

These are the foundations of the plant. They dig deep into the dirt giving stability, as well as sucking up nutrients.

Seaweed
Seaweed looks like a plant, but is an algae. It doesn't have roots, so it has to stick to rocks or float with the tide.

The petals attract insects and birds that collect pollen.

The stamen and carpels form the reproductive organs of a plant.

Flowers

Flowers are key to plant reproduction. They make pollen and develop seeds, and fruit.

Leaves

These are the work factories of the plant and capture the Sun's energy.

Water lily
The water lily's flat leaves float on the pond surface, as its roots sink into the pond bed.

weird or what?
The Venus flytrap doesn't just get its energy from the Sun. It also lures and feeds on unsuspecting insects. Yum!

What plant has the largest leaves?

Types of plants

Have a look around you. Not all plants are the same. But some plants are more similar than others.

Fern leaves unfurl as they grow.

Ferns

Ferns love damp and shady areas. They have prong-like leaves and spread using spores.

Most conifer trees keep their leaves all year round.

The sequoia is the largest tree in the world.

Moss

Mosses love moisture and grow in clumps. They don't have roots or grow flowers.

Conifers

Conifer trees grow cones that store their seeds. Most conifers have needle-shaped leaves.

There are about 12,000 species of moss.

You can identify a tree by the shape of its leaves.

Ash leaf

Maple leaf

Flowering plants

This is the biggest group of plants. They produce flowers, fruits and seeds, which mainly grow in seasonal cycles.

Scarlet oak leaf

Rainforest

These warm and wet forests are home to nearly half the world's plant species.

Deciduous

Deciduous plants shed their leaves to save food and survive drier seasons.

The raffia palm has leaves that grow up to 24 metres (79 feet) long.

How plants work

Plants have an amazing system for making and transporting food to all their different parts.

Photosynthesis

The green pigment chlorophyll traps sunlight in the leaves. The Sun's energy is then used to change water and carbon dioxide into sugar.

The Sun's energy is trapped in the leaves, and helps make food.

Cross-section through a leaf vein

Food is moved from leaves to roots and growing tips, along a set of tubes called phloem vessels.

A waste product of photosynthesis is oxygen, which animals need to survive.

Some water evaporates through tiny holes called stomata in the surface of the leaf. This process is called transpiration.

Tiny tubes called xylem vessels, carry water up the stem from the roots to the leaves.

Cross-section through a stem

Veins carry water around the leaf.

Roots suck water up from the ground.

Are plants the only organism to use photosynthesis?

New growth

Plants use sugar and starch as fuel. The fuel is transported to cells where it is burnt to release energy, which is used to grow new cells and repair old ones.

Wilting leaves

On warm, sunny days, plants lose lots of water from their leaves. If they lose too much their leaves collapse. This is called wilting. If plants don't get enough water their leaves will shrivel and die.

Desert plants

Plants that live in dry areas such as deserts have to save their water. Many have leaves that are thick and covered in wax to stop transpiration. Cacti have spines rather than leaves and thick stems in which they can store water.

Fruit acts as a store of sugar and water.

Carrot plants store food in their roots.

Bulb

Storing food

Spare food is stored for future use. Plants such as hyacinths store food in the base of their leaves. This makes the leaves swell and form a bulb. The bulb survives the winter and in spring it sprouts new leaves.

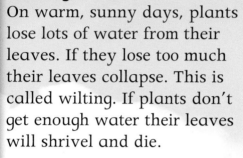

🤚 Get mucky 🤚

Place a stem of celery in a glass of water coloured with a few drops of food colouring. After two hours, cut across the stem. You will see tiny dots of colour showing the tubes that carry the water.

No, many bacteria also make food by photosynthesis.

Plant reproduction

Most plants start life as seeds. When the conditions are right they start to grow. As fully grown plants they make new seeds and the cycle starts again…

Stamens

Ovary

Petal

A flower's bright colours and sweet smell attract insects.

Pass the pollen

Pollen plays a vital part in plant reproduction. It looks like tiny pieces of dust and can be blown from flower to flower. It also sticks to insects and birds and gets flown to new flowers.

Fertilizing flowers

A flower has female parts that make eggs, or ova, and a ring of male parts, called stamens, which make pollen. Seeds develop when pollen fertilizes the female ova on another flower. This is called pollination.

Waving in the wind

A catkin is the flower of the willow tree. In catkins, the male and female parts are on separate flowers. Catkins move in the wind and release lots of pollen, which then pollinates the female flowers.

Bees carry pollen in sacs on their legs.

What is a spore?

Fruits and seeds

When a plant has been fertilized, the ovary swells up and becomes a fruit. There are many different types of fruit. Some are fleshy and sweet tasting, and others are dry and hard.

Nectarine

Pear

Plum

Seeds are enclosed within a fruit.

Fig

Scattering seeds

Plants scatter their seeds in different ways.

Dandelions have seeds with tiny parachutes that are carried by the wind.

Sycamore seeds have a wing that allows them to glide to the ground.

Burrs become attached to animal fur and get carried far away.

Animals eat fruits and drop the seeds on the ground.

New life

Seeds contain everything needed to grow a new plant. With enough food, water, and light the seed sprouts a root and baby stem, known as a shoot.

Shoot

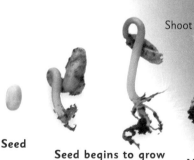

Seed

Seed begins to grow

Root

New plant forms

Running away

Not all new plants grow from seeds. The strawberry plant produces long stems, called runners, that grow along the ground. When the runner touches the ground, a new plantlet takes root and becomes a new plant.

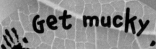

Get mucky

Make your own small garden inside a jar or tin. Fill it with some soil, then plant some seeds. Water them and watch them grow!

It is similar to a seed and plays the same role in fungi and algae life cycles.

What is an animal?

A key definition of an animal, as opposed to a plant, is that most animals can move voluntarily. Animals must also eat other living things to survive. Let's take a look at some of the things animals do.

Bald eagle

Food is fuel

All animals have to find and eat food to survive. Carnivores are animals that eat meat. Herbivores eat mainly plants. Omnivores are creatures that eat both plants and meat.

Squirrels eat seeds, nuts, fruit, and fungi.

Getting around

Many animals have muscles, which allow them to move in a variety of ways.

Flying: birds fly by flapping wings or gliding on currents of hot air.

Swimming: animals like fish swim by moving their bodies and fins.

Slithering: some snakes wriggle, others raise and flatten their bodies.

Walking and running: many animals walk and run using legs.

Reaching: sea anemones reach out their tentacles to sting prey.

What a nerve!

Animals have nerves, which carry information from their sense organs. Most animals have brains to monitor this information. The nerves also carry orders from the brain to the organs and muscles – such as instructions to stay still, attack, or run away!

How many species of animal are there on Earth?

Do animals talk?

Many animals are able to communicate with each other.

Most beetles will send "messages" to other beetles using special chemicals.

Pythons can go without food for months after one BIG meal!

Making babies

Most animals reproduce when a female egg is fertilized by a male sperm. Some animals give birth to babies, while others lay eggs.

Birds lay hard-shelled eggs, which hatch into chicks or ducklings.

Baby birds have to break out of the egg on their own.

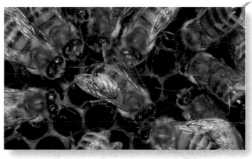

Honey bees constantly communicate. They give directions with a special dance.

Giraffes have seven vertebrae in their necks – the same as most other mammals. They are just much longer.

Monkeys scream at each other to sound an alarm.

27

Nobody knows the exact answer, but about 1.8 million have been identified.

Types of animals

There are so many different types, or species, of animals that scientists put them in groups so it's easier to study them. Mammals, birds, reptiles, amphibians, and fish are vertebrates. Creepy-crawlies are invertebrates.

Lizard

Tortoise

Reptiles

Most reptiles have dry, scaly skin. They mainly live on land. Nearly all reptiles lay eggs, but some give birth to babies.

Mammals

Mammals usually have live babies, which feed on their mother's milk when they're born. Mammals often have fur on their bodies. Humans are mammals.

Zebra

Wolf

Deer fawn

Mouse

Lion cub

What is the only mammal that can fly?

Birds

All birds have wings, and most (but not all) can fly. They have feathers and a beak. Baby birds hatch from eggs.

Parrot

Ostriches can run fast but can't fly.

Amphibians

Amphibians live both in water and on land. They usually have slimy skin. Baby amphibians hatch from jelly-like eggs.

Salamander

Frog

Fish

Fish need to live in water. They breathe through gills, and most are covered in scales. Fish use their fins to move through water.

Spineless creatures

Animals without backbones are called invertebrates. There are several types of invertebrates.

Insects, spiders, and crustaceans are part of the largest animal group.

Snails and slugs are part of an invertebrate group called gastropods.

Worms have long, soft bodies and no legs. They like damp areas.

Jellyfish, starfish, and sponges are invertebrates that live in water.

Octopus and squid live in the sea. They have eight arms.

Butterfly

Ladybird

Insects

There are more types of insects on Earth than any other animal. Insects can live almost anywhere. They have six legs and bodies with three sections.

Animal reproduction

Every kind of animal has young – this is called reproduction. Usually, it happens after males and females mate.

A mother macaque monkey holding her baby

Mammal reproduction

After animals mate, egg cells develop inside the mother. With mammals, the eggs develop fully into babies before she gives birth.

Zebra mother and baby

Helpless creatures

Monkeys and apes need years of nurturing before they can look after themselves.

An elephant develops inside its mother for two years!

Family ties

Elephants look after their young longer than any other animal apart from humans.

Become an expert...

on plant reproduction, pages **24–25**
on inheritance, pages **32–33**

Like all mammal babies, elephants drink milk from their mother.

Which animal lays the largest egg?

Babies from eggs

Most birds, fish, insects, and reptiles lay eggs. The number of eggs can range from one to millions!

A baby crocodile hatching out of its egg

Change and grow

Some animals, like butterflies, change enormously during their life cycle.

 A butterfly begins its life as an egg, which hatches into a tiny caterpillar.

 The caterpillar attaches itself to a twig and forms a hard outer shell.

 Inside the shell, the caterpillar changes and grows.

 The shell, which is often camouflaged, eventually splits open.

 A butterfly emerges. This process is known as metamorphosis.

Young and free

Once hatched in the sand, baby turtles have to find their own way into the sea.

Pouch babies

Female kangaroos have pouches on their tummy. After it's born, the tiny baby crawls into the pouch, where it stays for around three more months, feeding and growing.

Family ties

Female elephants stay with their family their whole lives. Males leave when they are around 13 years old.

Male emperor penguins look after the young while the females search for food.

The ostrich.

31

Inheritance

Your genes are a set of chemical instructions for building someone just like you. You inherit them from your parents, which is why you are like them in many ways. But unless you are a twin, your genes are unique.

Do you know what your DNA is?

DNA, when magnified, looks like a twisted ladder.

Tiny cells

Cells are the building blocks that make up all living things. Each cell in your body contains a complete set of genes – the information to make you as you are.

Chromosome

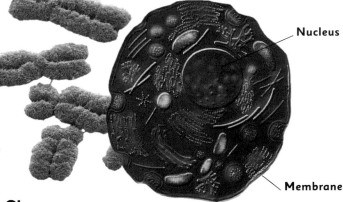

Nucleus

Membrane

Amazing DNA

DNA looks like a long, thin, twisted ropeladder. Each chromosome contains two metres of DNA. DNA is made up of four types of chemical units, which work like letters in an alphabet. Together they spell out a code that tells your cells how to make a human being.

Chromosomes

Your genes are organised into 46 chromosomes, arranged in 23 pairs. Genes and chromosomes are made from a chemical called DNA.

What is a gene?

Every cell in your body contains a set of 25,000 genes. All living things pass on their genes to their offspring. Sexual reproduction combines two sets of genes. You've got two of each gene, one from your mother and one from your father. Sometimes the gene from your mother comes into action, and other times your father's gene wins out.

You can only roll your tongue if the right gene is active.

What does DNA stand for?

Colour blindness

Some people have a gene which causes them to be colour blind. Look at the circle below. If you can see the number inside then you aren't colour blind.

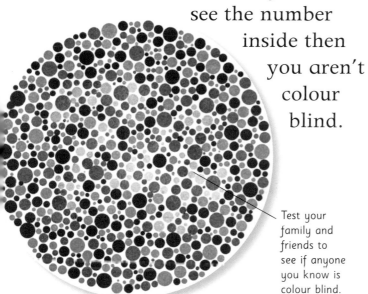

Test your family and friends to see if anyone you know is colour blind.

Seeing double

Identical twins share 100 per cent of their genes. A quarter of these are mirror twins which means that they are a mirror image of each other. For example, they might have an identical mole, but on the opposite arm to each other.

Who do you look like?

Children have a mixture of genes from their parents. This is why you might have your mum's eyes but your dad's smile!

This child has inherited her hair and skin colour from her mother.

The chromosomes of your father determine whether you will be a boy or a girl.

Become an expert...

on animal reproduction, pages 30–31

on health, pages 40–41

Deoxyribonucleic acid.

Bones and muscles

You would be like a lump of jelly without your skeleton – a frame of bones that holds you up and protects your internal organs.

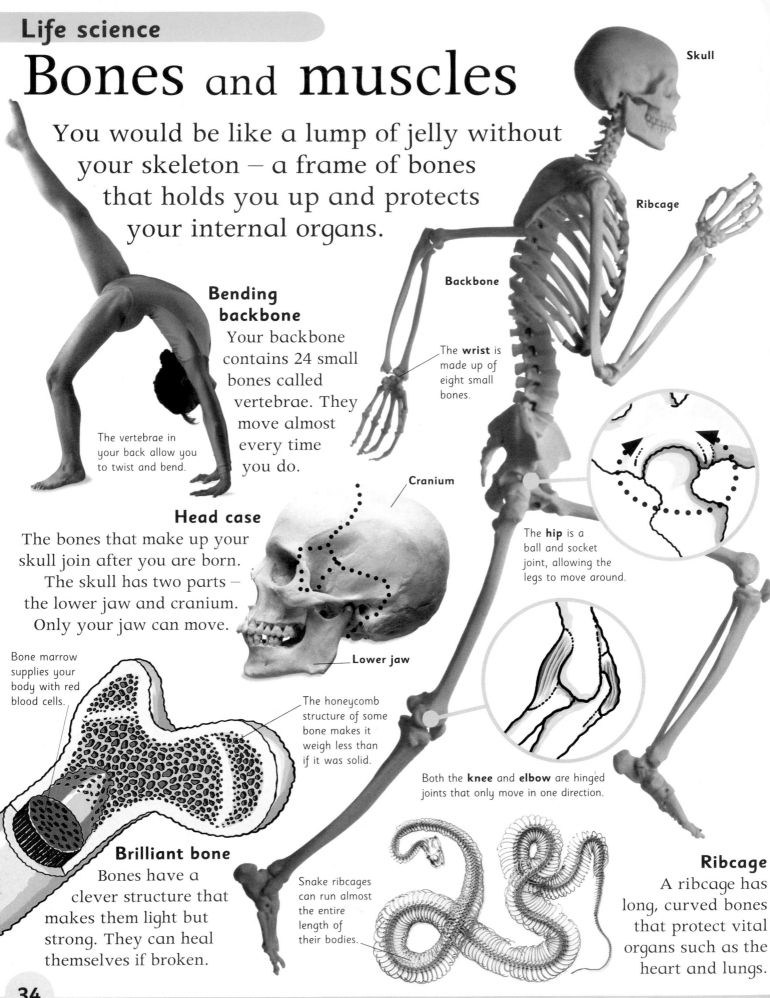

Skull

Ribcage

Backbone

Bending backbone

Your backbone contains 24 small bones called vertebrae. They move almost every time you do.

The vertebrae in your back allow you to twist and bend.

The **wrist** is made up of eight small bones.

Head case

The bones that make up your skull join after you are born. The skull has two parts – the lower jaw and cranium. Only your jaw can move.

Cranium

Lower jaw

The **hip** is a ball and socket joint, allowing the legs to move around.

Bone marrow supplies your body with red blood cells.

The honeycomb structure of some bone makes it weigh less than if it was solid.

Both the **knee** and **elbow** are hinged joints that only move in one direction.

Brilliant bone

Bones have a clever structure that makes them light but strong. They can heal themselves if broken.

Snake ribcages can run almost the entire length of their bodies.

Ribcage

A ribcage has long, curved bones that protect vital organs such as the heart and lungs.

How many bones does an adult human have?

Bending bits

Different kinds of joints all over your body keep you moving.

Thumbs have joints that allow them to rotate, which fingers cannot do.

Ankles contain different joints for up-and-down and side-to-side movement.

Wrists have a joint that allows them to turn but not go all the way round.

Neck bones feature a pivot joint that allows your head to turn.

Muscle magic

Muscles are rubbery, stretchy straps. You can control some of your muscles, like the muscles in your arms and legs. Others, such as your heart and bladder, operate without you having to think about it.

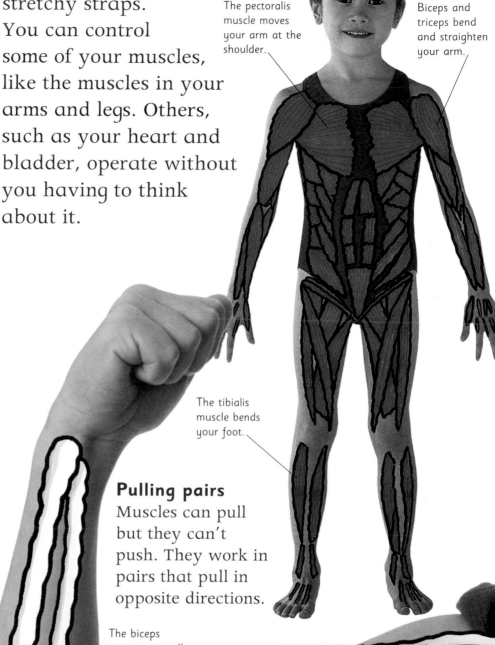

The pectoralis muscle moves your arm at the shoulder.

Biceps and triceps bend and straighten your arm.

The tibialis muscle bends your foot.

Making faces

Muscles in your face are attached to skin as well as bone. They allow you to make all kinds of expressions to show how you are feeling.

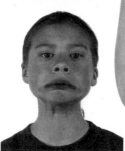

Pulling pairs

Muscles can pull but they can't push. They work in pairs that pull in opposite directions.

The biceps contract to pull the forearm up.

The triceps relax and stretch when the biceps contract.

Blood and breathing

Every few seconds you breathe in air.
Your lungs take out the oxygen and
send it into your blood. The blood
carries oxygen all round your body.

Liquid of life

Blood is made up of
cells floating in a liquid
called plasma. There
are three types of cells:

 Red blood cells, the
most common type of
blood cell, carry oxygen.

 White blood cells, which
are part of the immune
system, fight disease.

 Platelets help to
repair other cells if
they are damaged.

Your beating heart

Every time your
heart beats it pumps
blood around your
body. Half of the
heart sends blood
through your lungs.
The other half sends
blood around the
rest of your body.

Transport system

Blood travels around your
body in tubes called blood
vessels. Blood vessels
called arteries (red) carry
blood away from your
heart. Vessels called
veins (blue) carry blood
back to your heart.

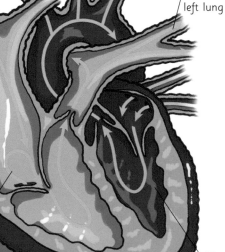

Arteries

Heart

Blood to all
parts of body

Veins

Blood to
left lung

Blood from
right lung

The right-hand
pump sends blood
to the lungs to
receive oxygen.

The left-hand
pump squirts
blood to the
organs and
muscles.

Blood from legs and feet

Blood to legs and feet

How many times does your heart beat every day?

Lungs

Your lungs fill most of the space inside your ribcage. They take in oxygen from the air and send out waste carbon dioxide.

No lungs

Not every animal has lungs. There are other ways animals breathe.

Frogs can absorb oxygen through their skin – even underwater.

Insects such as caterpillars breathe through body openings called spiracles.

Many sea creatures such as sharks breathe through gills.

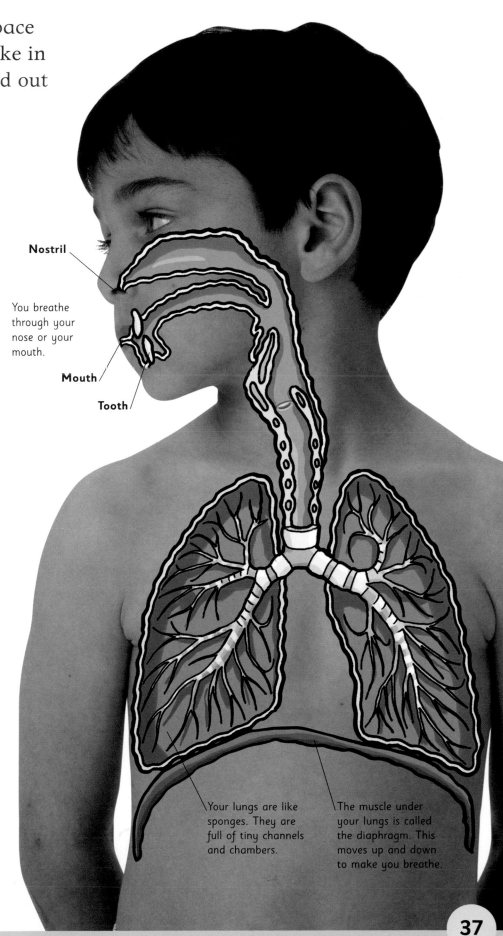

Nostril

You breathe through your nose or your mouth.

Mouth

Tooth

Your lungs are like sponges. They are full of tiny channels and chambers.

The muscle under your lungs is called the diaphragm. This moves up and down to make you breathe.

A child's heart beats between 130,000 and 170,000 times a day.

The digestion ride

Take a ride down your digestive system, as it breaks down your food to take out the nutrients and get rid of waste.

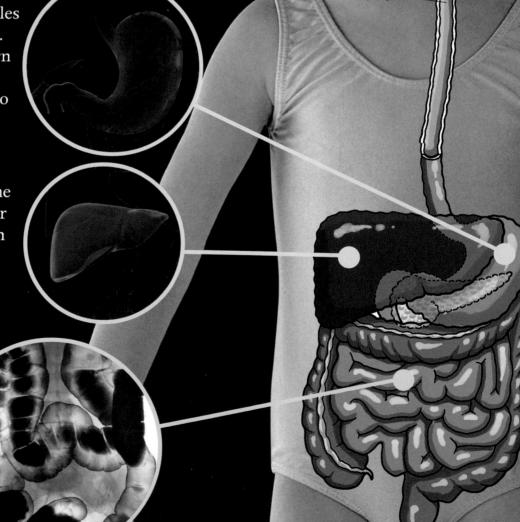

Mouth

First stop is the mouth. Saliva moistens the food to make it easier to chew and swallow. Food then heads down the oesophagus to your stomach.

Stomach

In your stomach, muscles churn the food around. Stomach acids help turn it into a semi-liquid before it is squirted into the intestines.

Liver

Your liver stores some vitamins and a sugar called glucose, which gives you energy.

Intestines

Your intestines are a long, tangled tube. The small intestine absorbs food into your bloodstream. The large intestine deals with undigested leftovers.

Oesophagus

Which is longer, your small intestine or your large intestine?

Super system
Cows have an amazing digestive system. There are four parts to a cow's stomach. Each one performs a different function to make sure food is digested and used in the most efficient way. Cows need this system to help them digest tough grass.

Stone eaters
Some birds eat grit. The tiny stones help digestion by breaking down food in the bird's stomach.

Food for health
You need to eat a variety of foods to keep your body working efficiently. A good diet includes a balance of food from each of the five food groups.

Carbohydrates, found in food such as bread, cereal, and potatoes.

Fats, which can be found in food such as oils. Fats give you energy.

Proteins, which can be found in eggs, fish, meat, dairy products, and nuts.

Minerals such as iron and calcium. Iron is found in some green vegetables.

Vitamins such as Vitamin C are found in fresh fruit and vegetables.

Kidneys
Your kidneys filter and clean your blood, taking out the chemicals that your body doesn't need. Kidneys also control the amount of water in your blood.

Waste disposal
Solid waste from the large intestine is stored in the rectum, and urine is stored in the bladder, until you are ready to go to the toilet.

weird or what?
Humans taste with their tongues – but other animals have different methods. Butterflies use their feet!

Your small intestine.

Health

Our way of life affects our health. Eating properly, exercising regularly, and getting enough sleep are all important for staying happy and fit.

A balanced diet

It is vital to eat a balance of the right foods. There are five major food groups and they all help your body in different ways.

5-a-day
You need to eat at least five portions of fruits and vegetables each day.

Fruit and vegetables
These foods provide you with vitamins and minerals as well as fibre. They help to prevent you becoming ill.

Meat, fish, and pulses
Protein repairs damaged cells. It should make up about 15 per cent of your daily diet.

Fats and sugars
Fat cushions the organs and transports some vitamins in your body.

Dairy products
Milk and dairy products provide you with calcium, necessary for bones, teeth, and muscles.

Drink up!
We can last quite a long time without food, but not without water. Water helps to digest food and flush out waste. Low water levels (dehydration) can cause headaches, dry skin, and tiredness.

You need to drink water frequently each day or you will dehydrate.

Which vitamin do we get from sunlight?

Ideally, children should be getting about 60 minutes of exercise a day.

Swimming is a good way of exercising all your muscles.

Keeping clean

Dirt contains harmful bacteria. Keeping clean helps you stay healthy.

Brushing your teeth in the morning and again before you go to bed.

Washing off the dirt with regular baths or showers.

Wearing clean clothes, especially clean pants and socks, each day.

Exercise

Exercise strengthens the muscles and heart, and encourages the production of special chemicals called endorphins. These make us feel good and act to reduce pain.

Many children relax more easily into sleep with a special cuddly toy.

Sleep

When you sleep, your body rests and your mind refreshes itself. When you are young you need a lot of sleep, but you need less as you get older.

Carbohydrates

Foods in this group include bread, pasta, and potatoes. Carbohydrates provide your body's energy. They should make up just over a third of your diet.

Read a book!

Health is not just about your body; it helps to have an active mind. Reading is a good activity because it stimulates your brain.

Become an expert...

on muscles, pages 34–35 on digestion, pages 38–39

A child needs between 10 and 12 hours sleep a night.

Vitamin D, which is important for strong bones.

Food chains

Everything in the living world needs food to survive. And everything must feed on something else. This is called a food chain. Each species is part of several different food chains.

Decomposers

At the start and end of every food chain there are decomposers, such as earthworms, fungi, and dung beetles. They help break down dead animals and plants, releasing the nutrients back into the soil.

Producers

Plants such as acacia trees or grasses get their energy from the Sun. They are known as producers.

Herbivores

Herbivores such as impala or zebra eat the plants. They do not eat meat.

What carnivorous plant catches and eats flies and spiders?

Scavengers

Dead meat is known as carrion and is eaten by scavengers such as hyenas, vultures, and bald eagles. These creatures rarely kill for food, they find animals that have died of natural causes and eat other animals' leftovers.

Carnivores

Carnivores only eat meat. On the African plains, carnivores include lions, leopards, and cheetahs.

A Venus flytrap.

Sea food

The further you go up the chain, the fewer animals there are. So in the sea, there are countless plankton, fewer fish, just a few seal, and even less polar bears.

Polar bear

Seal

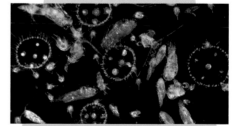

Fish

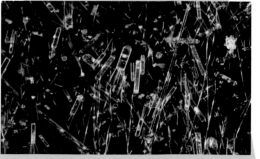

Zooplankton

Phytoplankton

Ecosystems

All over the world, living things exist in distinct kinds of places called ecosystems. Each has its own climate, soil, and complex community of plants and animals. Oceans and deserts have their own ecosystems.

Natural variety

There are different ecosystems all over the world, and the animals and plants in each one are adapted to its conditions.

Forests

Wherever there is enough rain, forests grow, and they provide homes for a huge range of plants and animals.

Oceans

More than 70 per cent of the Earth's surface is covered by ocean, which contains many different habitats.

Homes sweet homes

One ecosystem contains a number of habitats. A habitat is the natural home of a particular plant or animal. A tree, or even a leaf, can be a habitat.

Rivers and lakes

Freshwater ecosystems exist in pools, lakes, rivers, and streams. They are found over most of the world's land surface.

Become an expert...

on animal survival, pages 46–47
on the carbon cycle, pages 50–51

Polar and tundra

The freezing polar lands are at the far north and south of Earth, in the Arctic and Antarctic. At the edges farthest away from the poles, they merge into warmer tundra areas.

Are there any types of forest ecosystems other than tropical rainforests?

Mountains

Climate conditions change as you go up a mountain, so different ecosystems can exist here.

Seashores

Seashore ecosystems are half land and half sea. They change as the tide comes in and out.

Grasslands

Humans evolved in grassland habitats, and today, the largest and fastest land animals live here.

Deserts

They can be hot or cold, but deserts are always dry, with little rain. Only a few animals and plants survive here.

Trees offer shelter for animals, and food in the form of leaves and berries.

Insects feed on flowers, and pollinate them at the same time.

Living together

A group of living things in a habitat is called a community. Each one contains plants, animals, and other organisms that all rely on each other.

Frogspawn hatches into tadpoles. Some of these are eaten by other water creatures.

Rotting leaves and wood are home to fungi and small animals, such as beetles and slugs.

Snails feed on the leaves of plants, and provide food for other animals.

Ferns grow and absorb nutrients from the soil.

Frogs, which eat insects, live both on land and in the water.

Yes, deciduous woodlands and cold coniferous forests.

Staying alive

In order to survive, all animals and plants need food, water, shelter, and space. Each type of animal or plant has its own particular way of finding them.

Let's stick together
Clownfish and sea anemones live together and help each other (symbiosis). The sea anemone's tentacles can sting most fish, but the clownfish don't get hurt.

Camouflage
On the grasslands of Africa, lions try to creep up on their prey. They can hide in the long grass because they are the same colour. This is called camouflage.

Long-eared bat with a moth

Night hunter
Some animals hunt for food at night. The long-eared bat uses sound to find insects in the dark. It makes a squeaking noise and listens to the echo as the noise bounces back off objects. It can tell exactly where an insect is.

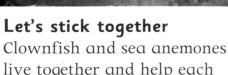
A huge worm is only enough food to keep a shrew going for a few hours.

All-day hunter
Some animals have to hunt for food day and night. Shrews need to eat 80 to 90 per cent of their body weight every day to survive. These animals are tiny, but aggressive.

A tapeworm is a kind of parasite. Where does it live?

The tiny Arctic tern makes a long migration. It flies between the North and South Poles each year.

Great travellers

When food and water become scarce in one place or the weather gets too cold, animals may move home (migrate). Some animals migrate every year.

Parasites

Some organisms, called parasites, live on or inside the bodies of other organisms, which they feed on. Caterpillars live as parasites on plants.

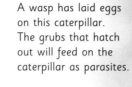

A wasp has laid eggs on this caterpillar. The grubs that hatch out will feed on the caterpillar as parasites.

Pack of wolves

Wolves live and hunt in groups called packs. This is safer than living alone and makes it easier to hunt larger animals.

House builders

Many animals build homes for themselves to provide shelter from predators and bad weather.

Birds make nests out of mud or twigs, often hidden away in trees or bushes.

Burrows dug into the soil are used by animals such as rabbits and badgers.

Beavers pile up sticks in rivers to make a nest with an underwater entrance.

Wasps chew up wood to make soggy paper, which they then shape into nests.

Big hunger

Elephants have big appetites. A hungry elephant will push over a whole tree and eat every leaf and twig to satisfy its hunger.

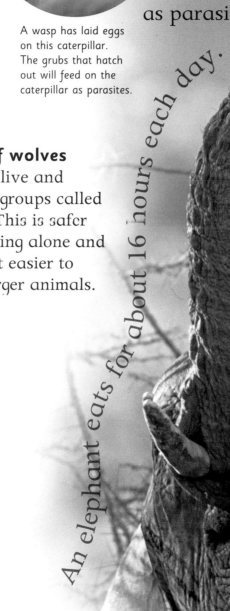

An elephant eats for about 16 hours each day.

Inside the human body, feeding on food you've swallowed.

Earth's cycles

Everything in nature is recycled. Living things take in oxygen, nitrogen, carbon, and water and use them to live. When they die and decompose, the substances they are made of are used again.

Nitrogen cycle

All living things need nitrogen. Plants take in nitrogen from the soil. Animals get nitrogen from eating plants. When animals and plants die they put nitrogen back into the soil.

At night, plants take in oxygen and give out carbon dioxide.

CARBON DIOXIDE

OXYGEN

Bacteria plays an important role in the nitrogen cycle. They change nitrogen into the form plants can use. Without bacteria plants would die of nitrogen starvation.

Nitrogen gas is abundant in our atmosphere.

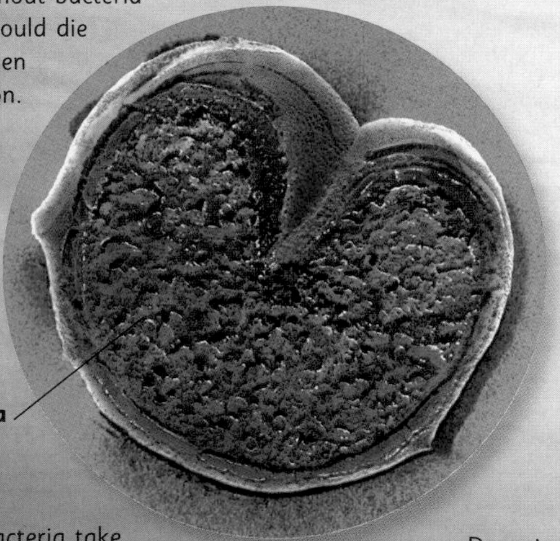

Bacteria

Other bacteria take in nitrates and release nitrogen back into the atmosphere.

Decaying animals and plants put nitrogen back into the soil.

Animals eat plants containing nitrates.

Do you think there is more oxygen or nitrogen in our atmosphere?

During the day, plants take in carbon dioxide and give out oxygen.

CARBON DIOXIDE

OXYGEN

From our atmosphere to Earth

During an electrical storm, some nitrogen is washed out of the atmosphere and falls to the ground. Plants can then draw the nitrogen in through their roots.

Oxygen cycle

Animals take in oxygen and use it to release energy from their food. It is put back into the air by green plants during photosynthesis. Algae and plankton do the same job in water.

Animals breathe in oxygen and breathe out carbon dioxide all the time.

OXYGEN

CARBON DIOXIDE

Our atmosphere contains 21 per cent oxygen and 78 per cent nitrogen.

All living things

Every living thing contains carbon. Human beings take in carbon through carbohydrates, fats, and proteins in food, and release it as carbon dioxide gas when breathing out. It is also released from dead matter, sometimes quite soon, sometimes millions of years later in fuels like oil and coal.

Carbon cycle

Green plants take in the gas carbon dioxide from the air and use it to make food, converting it into things such as carbohydrates. Animals take in some of the carbon when they eat plants.

Animals

Animals such as these sheep contribute to the carbon cycle by eating, breathing, and dropping waste. They take in carbon in the plants they eat, and release it when they breathe out. Their bodies will release more carbon when they die.

Carbon dioxide in the atmosphere

CARBON DIOXIDE

OXYGEN

CARBON

CARBON DIOXIDE RELEASED

Animals breathe out carbon dioxide.

Animals eat plants and take in some carbon.

An animal's droppings also contribute to the carbon cycle.

50

In particular circumstances, carbon forms a hard crystal. What is its name?

Plants and animals die and their bodies decay.

DECOMPOSING

Fossil fuels
Sometimes the remains of organisms are exposed to extreme pressure and heat. Over millions of years, they turn into carbon-rich fuels, like coal and oil.

Waste disposal
When animals die, their bodies break down and decompose.

DECOMPOSING

Waste fertiliser
Part of you might once have been part of a dinosaur. Why? Because like all living things, dinosaurs produced waste and their waste became a part of the never-ending carbon cycle.

DECOMPOSING

Digesters
Decomposition in the soil is helped along by the endless action of worms and bacteria. These animals are an important part of the carbon cycle.

A diamond.

What's the matter?

Everything around you is made of matter, even the things you can't see. But everything looks and acts differently – that's because matter has different forms.

Solid, liquid or gas

The most common states of matter are solid, liquid and gas. Each state behaves differently because the particles in their make up move in different ways.

Four states

There are four main states of matter.

Solids have a definite shape. Most of them are hard, like rock.

Liquids take on the shape of their container, and have a fixed volume.

Gases have no fixed shape. They fill any space they are in, such as a balloon.

Plasma exists at very high temperatures, like inside the Sun.

Nearly everything on Earth is solid, liquid, or gas.

Planet Earth
Earth has a solid core, surrounded by liquid rock, which the solid crust floats on. Liquid water covers most of the crust and a layer of gas called the atmosphere surrounds the planet.

The blue areas are the oceans, which are liquid water.

Clouds form from water vapour (a gas) in the atmosphere.

The green areas are land, which is made of solid rocks.

Which forms of matter are humans?

Using gas
When air in a balloon is heated, it becomes lighter than the surrounding air and quickly fills the balloon. The lighter air rises, taking the balloon and passengers with it.

No matter
A place with no matter, not even air, is called a vacuum. The closest thing to a vacuum is the space between stars.

Astronauts wear special suits in space because it is very cold and there is no air to breathe.

Curiosity quiz
Look through the Polar Regions pages and see if you can identify the picture clues below.

Become an expert...
on amazing atoms, pages **58–59**
on the Universe, pages **94–95**

We are three forms, our bones are solid, our blood is liquid, and we breathe air.

Properties of matter

What they are...

There are many different properties of matter.

Boiling point is the hottest a liquid can get before becoming a gas.

Freezing point is the temperature at which a liquid becomes a solid.

Plasticity is how well a solid can be reshaped.

Conductivity is how well a material lets electricity or heat travel through it.

Malleability is how well a solid can be shaped without breaking.

Tensile strength is how much a material can stretch without breaking.

Flammability is how easily and quickly a substance will catch fire.

Reflectivity is how well a material reflects light. Water reflects well.

Transparency is how well a material will let light pass through it.

Flexibility is how easily a material can be bent.

Solubility is how well a substance will dissolve, such as salt in water.

Some materials are hard and brittle, while others are flexible. Some materials are colourful, while others are transparent. These kinds of features are called "properties".

A cork floats on oil. Oil floats on water.

Does it float?

It's easy to learn about some properties, such as the ability to float. The amount of matter in a certain volume of an object is called its density. Objects and liquids float on liquids of a higher density and sink through liquids of a lower density.

A plastic building brick sinks through oil but floats on water.

An onion sinks through oil and water, but floats on syrup. Syrup sinks below water.

A good insulator

Heat cannot easily pass through some materials. These are known as insulators. For example aerogel can completely block the heat of a flame. But don't try this at home!

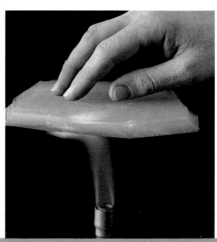

Is diamond harder than quartz?

Broken window

Brittleness

Some materials, such as window glass, are particularly brittle. They will break when pushed out of shape even a small amount.

Hardness

A scientist called Friedrich Mohs created a scale of ten minerals to compare how hard they are. Many materials are graded on this scale.

Compressibility

Gases can be squashed, or compressed, by squeezing more into the same space. This is what happens when you pump up a tyre.

Gas can be compressed because its particles are far apart. A bicycle pump pushes the particles closer together.

Foot pump

Gas particles

Diamond is the hardest mineral.

9 Corundum

10 Diamond

8 Topaz

7 Quartz

6 Feldspar

5 Apatite

4 Fluorite

3 Calcite

2 Gypsum

1 Talc

Softest mineral

Get mucky

Collect some different pebbles and put them in order of hardness. A pebble is harder than another if it scratches it. This is how Mohs worked out his scale.

A smooth flow

Some liquids flow more easily than others. It depends on their "stickiness", or viscosity. Hot lava from a volcano flows slowly because it is sticky.

Yes, a diamond is the hardest mineral of all. It will scratch quartz.

Liquid metal

Every substance melts and boils at a particular temperature (its melting and boiling points). Most metals are solid at everyday temperatures because they have a high melting point. But mercury has such a low melting point that it is liquid even at room temperature.

Condensation

As water vapour in the air is cooled, it changes into liquid water. This is called condensation. You can see it on the outside of a cold bottle.

When water vapour in the air touches a cold bottle, it condenses into tiny drops of liquid.

Changing states

When solids get hot enough, they melt and become liquids. When liquids get cold enough, they freeze and become solid. This is called changing states and it happens to all kinds of substances.

Changing states of water

Water exists as a solid, liquid, or gas. You can find all three forms of water in your home. They are ice, water, and steam (water vapour).

Ice is solid water. It forms when liquid is cooled until it freezes. Each piece of ice has a definite shape.

When ice is warmed, it melts and becomes liquid and takes on the shape of the container holding it.

As water is heated, bubbles of steam form. They rise to the surface and burst, so steam escapes into the air.

Rivers of iron

Iron must be heated in a furnace to make it melt. Molten iron is so hot it glows white. It is poured into a mould and left to harden to make solid iron objects.

Why does chocolate become soft and gooey in your mouth?

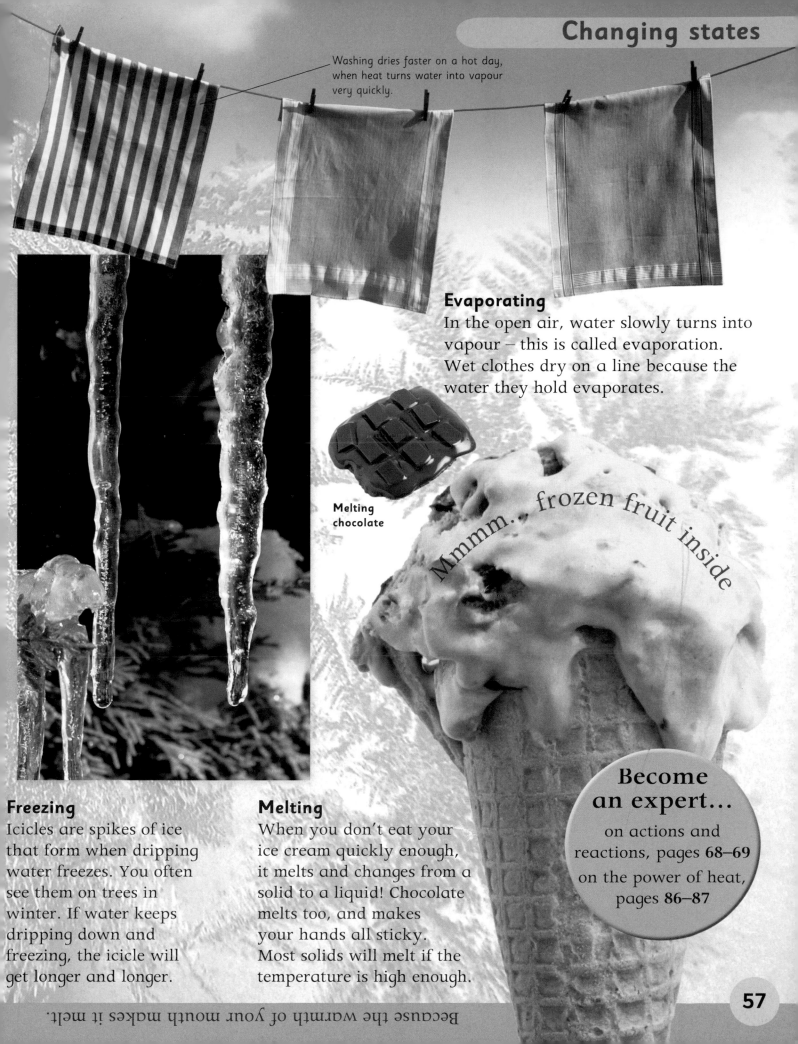

Washing dries faster on a hot day, when heat turns water into vapour very quickly.

Evaporating

In the open air, water slowly turns into vapour – this is called evaporation. Wet clothes dry on a line because the water they hold evaporates.

Melting chocolate

Mmmm... frozen fruit inside

Freezing

Icicles are spikes of ice that form when dripping water freezes. You often see them on trees in winter. If water keeps dripping down and freezing, the icicle will get longer and longer.

Melting

When you don't eat your ice cream quickly enough, it melts and changes from a solid to a liquid! Chocolate melts too, and makes your hands all sticky. Most solids will melt if the temperature is high enough.

Become an expert...

on actions and reactions, pages **68–69**

on the power of heat, pages **86–87**

Because the warmth of your mouth makes it melt.

Amazing atoms

If you could keep smashing an object into smaller and smaller bits, you would eventually break it down into bits that can't get any smaller – atoms. Atoms are tiny particles that make up everything around us.

Electrons whizz around the nucleus of the atom

Inside an atom

Inside an atom are three tiny types of particle: protons, neutrons, and electrons. Protons and neutrons make up the atom's nucleus (core). The electrons are outside this.

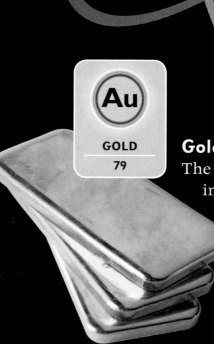

Neutron

Proton

Electron

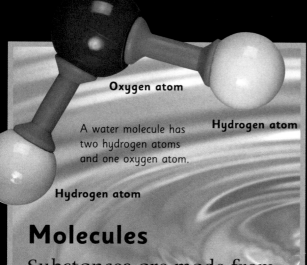

Oxygen atom

A water molecule has two hydrogen atoms and one oxygen atom.

Hydrogen atom

Hydrogen atom

Molecules

Substances are made from little groups of atoms called molecules. The molecules in water have three atoms.

Au

GOLD

79

Golden number

The number of protons in an atom is called its atomic number. The atomic number of gold is 79. This means that each gold atom has 79 protons.

How many atoms are there in a drop of water?

Sunflower oil comes from the seeds that grow in the middle of a sunflower.

Oxygen atom

Big molecules

In natural substances like vegetable oil, the atoms are often joined in chains to make very large molecules. The molecules in sunflower oil contain 50 atoms each.

Hydrogen atom

Carbon atom

weird or what?

An atom is mostly empty space. If an atom were the size of a sports stadium, the nucleus would be the size of a marble in the middle.

The explosion of a nuclear bomb can create a spectacular "mushroom cloud".

The mighty atom

When the nucleus of an atom is split, it releases a huge amount of energy. Nuclear bombs use this "atomic energy" to create huge explosions. Nuclear power stations use the energy to produce electricity.

There's about 5 sextillion (5,000,000,000,000,000,000,000,000,000,000).

Molecules

In most materials, atoms are joined in tiny groups called molecules. The shapes of molecules and the way they pack together can help explain how different materials behave.

Frozen solid

Cold molecules move slowly, allowing them to pack together more easily. When water freezes, the molecules line up in neat rows, forming ice crystals.

Steaming ahead

Molecules are always jiggling about. When they get hot, they move further and faster. When water heats up, the molecules may start moving so fast that they escape into the air as water vapour.

Snow may look like white powder, but if you look closely you can see thousands of tiny crystals as clear as glass.

Clouds appear when water vapour cools down and becomes liquid again. The grey mist is made of millions of tiny liquid droplets.

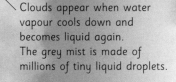

Melt: As a solid heats up, its molecules move faster until they break free from each other and move separately, turning the solid into a liquid.

Liquid

Solid

Solidify: As a liquid cools, its molecules lose energy and move more slowly. Eventually they start sticking together, turning the liquid into a solid.

If a liquid is poured into a jar or bottle, it takes the shape of its container and stays in place.

Are diamonds impossible to destroy?

Diamond is made into jewels that are almost indestructible.

Diamond molecule

Diamond is the hardest natural substance known. Its hardness comes from the way the carbon atoms in diamond are arranged. Each atom is joined by strong bonds to four neighbouring atoms.

Each group of five atoms in diamond forms a pyramid shape. This shape makes diamond amazingly strong.

Become an expert...

on changing states, pages 56–57

on minerals, pages 104–105

Graphite molecule

Graphite, like diamond, is also made of carbon atoms, but the atoms are arranged in a different way, making graphite very soft.

Each carbon atom in graphite is joined to only three neighbours. The atoms form layers that slip over each other, making graphite soft.

Graphite is used to make the soft lead in pencils.

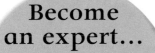

Evaporate: As a liquid heats up, its molecules speed up until they move fast enough to float away as gas.

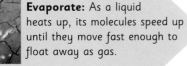

Condense: When gas molecules lose energy and slow down, they stick together and form liquid.

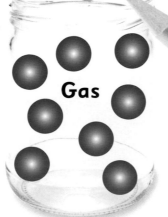

Gas

A gas can fill any container it's put in. If there's no lid to seal the container, the gas will escape into the air.

No, you can burn them.

Elements

An element is a chemical made up of just one type of atom. Scientists have discovered 117 different elements. The chart on this page, called the periodic table, shows most of them.

The elements in our bodies come from what we eat.

The periodic table

In the periodic table, elements are arranged by the number of protons in their atoms, starting with hydrogen. Elements with similar properties fall into groups, which are shown in colour.

1	2	3	4	5	6	7	8	9
H HYDROGEN 1								
Li LITHIUM 3	**Be** BERYLLIUM 4							
Na SODIUM 11	**Mg** MAGNESIUM 12							
K POTASSIUM 19	**Ca** CALCIUM 20	**Sc** SCANDIUM 21	**Ti** TITANIUM 22	**V** VANADIUM 23	**Cr** CHROMIUM 24	**Mn** MANGANESE 25	**FE** IRON 26	**Co** COBALT 27
Rb RUBIDIUM 37	**Sr** STRONTIUM 38	**Y** YTTRIUM 39	**Zr** ZIRCONIUM 40	**Nb** NIOBIUM 41	**Mo** MOLYBDENUM 42	**Tc** TECHNETIUM 43	**Ru** RUTHENIUM 44	**Rh** RHODIUM 45
Cs CAESIUM 55	**Ba** BARIUM 56	LANTHANIDES or RARE-EARTH METALS 57 – 71	**Hf** HAFNIUM 72	**Ta** TANTALUM 73	**W** TUNGSTEN 74	**Re** RHENIUM 75	**Os** OSMIUM 76	**Ir** IRIDIUM 77
Fr FRANCIUM 87	**Ra** RADIUM 88	ACTINIDES or RARE-EARTH RADIOACTIVE METALS 89 – 103	**Rf** RUTHERFORDIUM 104	**Db** DUBNIUM 105	**Sg** SEABORGIUM 106	**Bh** BOHRIUM 107	**Hs** HASSIUM 108	**Mt** MEITNERIUM 109

Each vertical column is called a GROUP, or family, of elements. Some groups have elements sharing very similar properties. Other groups have elements with less in common.

La LANTHANUM 57	**Ce** CERIUM 58	**Pr** PRASEODYMIUM 59	**Nd** NEODYMIUM 60	**Pm** PROMETHIUM 61	**Sm** SAMARIUM 62
Ac ACTINIUM 89	**Th** THORIUM 90	**Pa** PROTACTINIUM 91	**U** URANIUM 92	**Np** NEPTUNIUM 93	**Pu** PLUTONIUM 94

Milk contains the element calcium, which helps form your teeth and bones.

This bucket is made of the element iron coated with the element zinc, which stops iron rusting.

Metal and non-metals

Most elements are metals, and the others are called non-metals. Metals are normally solid, shiny, and hard. They all conduct electricity and heat. Silver, aluminium, and zinc are metals. Carbon, oxygen, and silicon are non-metals.

What is the main element used to make nuclear bombs?

Every element has a name, a symbol made of one or two letters, and an atomic number. The atomic number is the number of protons in one atom of the element.

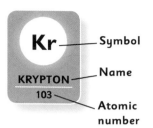

Oxygen is the most important gas. We take oxygen from the air we breathe.

Kr — Symbol

KRYPTON — Name

103 — Atomic number

18

He
HELIUM
2

13 **14** **15** **16** **17**

B BORON 5
C CARBON 6
N NITROGEN 7
O OXYGEN 8
F FLUORINE 9
Ne NEON 10

Al ALUMINIUM 13
Si SILICON 14
P PHOSPHORUS 15
S SULPHUR 16
Cl CHLORINE 17
Ar ARGON 18

10 **11** **12**

Ni NICKEL 28
Cu COPPER 29
Zn ZINC 30
Ga GALLIUM 31
Ge GERMANIUM 32
As ARSENIC 33
Se SELENIUM 34
Br BROMINE 35
Kr KRYPTON 36

Pd PALLADIUM 46
Ag SILVER 47
Cd CADMIUM 48
In INDIUM 49
Sn TIN 50
Sb ANTIMONY 51
Te TELLURIUM 52
I IODINE 53
Xe XENON 54

Pt PLATINUM 78
Au GOLD 79
Hg MERCURY 80
Tl THALLIUM 81
Pb LEAD 82
Bi BISMUTH 83
Po POLONIUM 84
At ASTATINE 85
Rn RADON 86

Ds DARMSTADTIUM 110
Rg ROENTGENIUM 111

Eu EUROPIUM 63
Gd GADOLINIUM 64
Tb TERBIUM 65
Dy DYSPROSIUM 66
Ho HOLMIUM 67
Er ERBIUM 68
Tm THULIUM 69
Yb YTTERBIUM 70
Lu LUTETIUM 71

Am AMERICIUM 95
Cm CURIUM 96
Bk BERKELIUM 97
Cf CALIFORNIUM 98
Es EINSTEINIUM 99
Fm FERMIUM 100
Md MENDELEVIUM 101
No NOBELIUM 102
Lr LAWRENCIUM 103

KEY:

Alkali metals: These silvery metals are very reactive.

Alkaline-earth metals: These shiny, silvery white metals are reactive.

Transition metals: Many are strong and have high boiling and melting points.

Lanthanides: Many are soft, shiny, and silvery-white metals.

Actinides: These are radioactive heavy elements.

Poor metals: Softer, weaker metals.

Non-metals: Most are gases at room temperature and easily snap as solids.

Halogens: These non-metals are highly reactive and harmful.

Noble gases: These non-metals are the least reactive of all the elements.

Become an expert... on elements, pages 64–65 on electricity, pages 76–77

Useful elements

We use elements to make all sorts of useful or decorative objects.

Gold is a precious metal. It is used to make jewellery.

Copper is a metal that conducts electricity well. It is used in electrical wires.

Silicon is a non-metal used to make the chips that power computers.

Carbon fibres are strong but light, so they are used for tennis rackets.

Iron is a strong, silvery metal. It is magnetic and has many uses.

Aluminium is a soft, shiny metal. It is used to make drinks cans.

Sulphur is a yellow non-metal used to harden rubber to make tyres.

Titanium is a lightweight metal and a small amount is used in aeroplanes.

Helium is a gas used in balloons because it is lighter than air.

Chlorine is a yellow-green gas, used in bleach and to make some plastics.

Mercury is a liquid metal used in dental fillings. It was once used in thermometers.

Properties of elements

Alkali metals

These are soft, lightweight metals that react easily with other chemicals, such as water. When put in water they fizz and pop violently. Sodium is an alkali metal. It reacts with the gas chlorine to form common salt.

Transition metals

This group includes well-known and useful metals.

Silver is used in medals, ornaments, jewellery, and cutlery (knives and forks).

Zinc protects things from rusting. One of its many uses is in the casing of batteries.

Nickel is used in silver-coloured coins because it does not lose its shine.

Titanium is lightweight yet incredibly strong. It is used to repair bones and joints.

In the periodic table, elements with similar properties are arranged in groups. Some groups are made up of elements that react easily with other chemicals to form new compounds. Other groups include elements that barely react with anything at all.

What are transition metals?

Forty elements make up a group known as the transition metals. These are typical metals, being solid, shiny, and mostly hard. The precious metals gold, silver, and platinum are in this group.

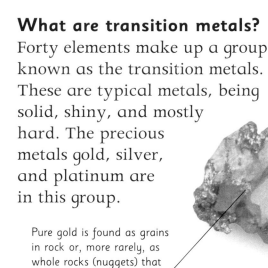

Pure gold is found as grains in rock or, more rarely, as whole rocks (nuggets) that are worth a small fortune.

Precious metals like gold are long-lasting because they react poorly with other chemicals. Gold is one of the least reactive elements.

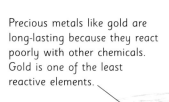

Which element is the most valuable precious metal?

Calcium is an
alkaline-earth metal.
It is found in seashells
as calcium carbonate.

The dazzling light
of fireworks comes
from burning
magnesium.

Alkaline-earth metals

Five elements, including magnesium and
calcium, are called alkaline-earth metals.
Like alkali metals, they are soft and light.
They don't react as strongly with water,
but they join with other chemicals to make
many compounds important in nature.

Noble gases

The six noble gases get
their name because
they hardly react with
other chemicals, as
though staying aloof.
They include neon and
argon, which are used
to make lasers and
coloured lights.

Poor metals

The elements in this group
are soft and weak. They
arc called poor metals
but are very useful. Tin,
lead, and aluminium are
examples of poor metals.

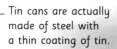

Tin cans are actually
made of steel with
a thin coating of tin.

Chlorine smells strongly and can sting your eyes.

Halogens

Five elements make up a group
called the halogens. These are
all highly reactive chemicals.
The gas chlorine is one of the
best-known halogens. It
is added to the water in
swimming pools because
it kills germs.

Rhodium. It is about ten times more expensive than gold.

65

Mixtures and compounds

Mixture of milk and cereal

When diffcrent elements bond together in a chemical reaction, they form a compound. But when chemicals mix together without bonding, they simply form a mixture. Mixtures are much easier to separate than compounds.

Colorado River, Arizona, USA

Suspension
A muddy river is a type of mixture called a suspension. Small particles of soil are "suspended" in the water, making it brown and cloudy.

Alloy
Different types of metal can be melted and mixed together to make a kind of mixture called an alloy. The alloy has different properties from the original metals. This tankard is made of pewter, which is an alloy of tin and lead. Pewter is much harder than tin or lead.

Pewter tankard

Salt forming on the shore of the Dead Sea in Jordan.

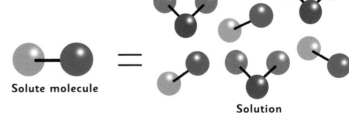

Water + Solute molecule = Solution

Solution
If you stir sugar into water, the sugar molecules spread out and fit between the water molecules, making the sugar seem to disappear. We say the sugar (a solute) has dissolved in the water (a solvent). This kind of mixture is called a solution. Sea water is a solution of water and salt. If you let sea water dry out, the salt reappears.

What is an 18-carat gold ring made of?

Cream and cheese are made by separating milk.

Separating compounds

It takes a great deal of effort to separate a compound into pure elements. To make pure iron, you have to separate the compound iron oxide into iron and oxygen. This is done in a very hot blast furnace.

Iron ore (rock rich in iron oxide)

Pure iron

Separating mixtures

A mixture can be easily separated in several ways.

Evaporation removes water from a mixture by turning it into a gas (water vapour).

Filtration separates large particles, such as coffee grinds, from a liquid.

Spinning separates liquids from solids. Spin dryers help dry clothes this way.

Distillation separates mixtures of liquids by making them evaporate and condense.

Milk

Strawberries and cream

Separating milk

Whole milk can be separated into cream and skimmed milk by spinning it in a bowl. The heavier skimmed milk spins away from the lighter cream, which stays in the centre of the spinning bowl.

67

Reactions and changes

When the atoms in molecules rearrange to form new kinds of molecules, we say a chemical reaction has taken place. Chemical reactions often lead to a dramatic change.

Melting is not a chemical reaction.

Chemical change

Fire is caused by a chemical reaction. When wood burns, the atoms in wood are rearranged to form new kinds of molecules. This process releases energy as light and heat, producing glowing flames.

Burning is a chemical reaction.

Physical change

Not all dramatic changes are caused by chemical reactions. When ice lollies melt, the atoms in the water molecules do not get rearranged into new molecules – they remain water molecules. Melting is simply a physical change.

Escaping energy
Chemical reactions can release energy as heat and light. A sparkler contains chemicals that release a lot of energy as light to create a dazzling shower of sparks.

What chemical reaction makes silver objects slowly turn grey and dull?

Speeding up reactions

Cooking makes carrots softer because the heat causes a chemical reaction. Chopping carrots into small bits speeds up the reaction because it increases the area of contact between the carrots and the hot water.

Sliced carrots cook faster than whole carrots.

Glow in the dark

Light sticks glow in the dark thanks to a chemical reaction that releases energy as light. You can slow down this reaction by putting a light stick in a fridge, which makes it last longer.

Get mucky

Ask an adult to boil some red cabbage and save the coloured water. Let the water cool. Then add acid (vinegar) or alkalki (bicarbonate) and watch for a spectacular change of colour!

Soda volcano

If you drop mints into a bottle of fizzy drink, the drink turns to foam and explodes out in an instant. This is a physical change rather than a chemical reaction. The rough surface of the mints helps gas, dissolved in the drink, to turn into bubbles much more quickly than it normally would.

Tarnishing. It happens when silver atoms react with oxygen atoms in air.

Irreversible changes

Nylon jacket

Physical changes like freezing are easy to reverse: you can freeze water and then melt the ice to make water again. Most chemical reactions, however, are very difficult to reverse because they create new kinds of molecules.

Cooking

When food is cooked, heat triggers chemical reactions that change it permanently. When a freshly baked cake cools down, it doesn't turn back into gooey cake mixture.

Manmade materials

Chemical reactions can be used to create new materials that don't exist in nature. Nylon, for example, is a fabric made using chemicals from oil. Many types of clothes from socks to coats are made of nylon.

Baking powder

Baking powder makes cakes light and fluffy. It contains chemicals that react when they're wet to produce bubbles of gas.

Rotting

Rotting food is full of tiny organisms such as a bacteria and fungi. These organisms trigger chemical reactions that break down food molecules, changing them permanently.

A fresh pepper looks plump and brightly coloured.

An old pepper darkens and shrivels up as it rots.

Why are some parts of cars covered with a layer of shiny chrome (chromium)?

Ready to fall

Maple trees shed their leaves in autumn. Before the leaves die, they change from green to golden, orange, or red. The colour changes because a chemical reaction in the leaves destroys the green substance (chlorophyll) inside leaf cells.

Maple leaves turn orange as they die.

Become an expert...

on plants, pages 20–21
on ecosystems, pages 44–45

Solid as a rock

Concrete is made by mixing gravel, sand, cement powder, and water. A chemical reaction between the water and cement makes the mixture harden permanently to become as solid as rock – ideal for building dams.

Rust

Iron reacts chemically with oxygen in the air to form rust – a flaky, reddish-brown compound. Rust can ruin cars, so the metal is painted to protect it.

Severe rust

The chrome protects the iron underneath from rusting.

What is energy?

Energy is what makes everything happen. Your body needs energy so that you can move, grow, and keep warm. We also need energy to power our cars, light our homes, and do thousands of other jobs.

Sunshine

We get nearly all our energy from the Sun. Plants absorb the energy in sunlight and store it as chemical energy. The stored energy enters our bodies as food and is released inside our body's cells. All animals and plants obtain their energy from the Sun this way.

Only a tiny fraction of the Sun's energy reaches Earth.

Sources of energy

Energy comes from lots of different sources.

Wind drives wind turbines, which convert movement energy into electricity.

Geothermal energy is heat from deep underground.

Plants can be burnt to provide energy for cooking, heating, and lighting.

Waves can be used to make small amounts of electricity.

Dams harness the energy in rivers flowing downhill to make electricity.

The Sun's energy can be captured by solar panels to make electricity.

Fossil fuels such as oil are used to power cars and to make electricity.

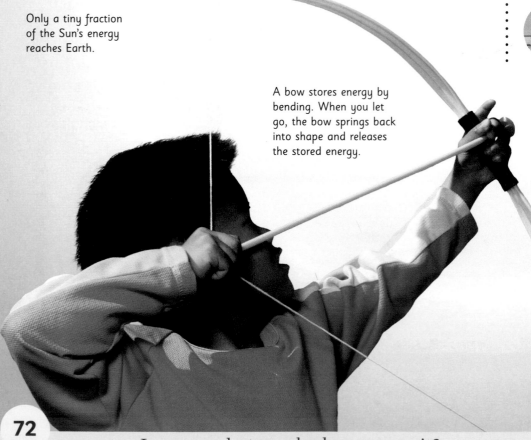

A bow stores energy by bending. When you let go, the bow springs back into shape and releases the stored energy.

Stored energy

An object can store energy and release it later. When you wind up a clockwork toy, energy is stored in a spring. A bow and arrow uses stored energy to shoot the arrow. Stored energy is also called potential energy because it has the potential to make things happen.

Is energy destroyed when we use it?

Movement energy

Rollercoasters start from the top of a hill, where their height gives them a lot of potential energy. As they move downhill, the potential energy turns into movement energy (kinetic energy), making them go faster and faster.

Nuclear energy

Matter is made up of tiny particles called atoms. The centre of an atom, called a nucleus, stores huge amounts of energy. This nuclear energy is used in power stations to make electricity.

Electrical energy

Lightning is caused by electrical energy in a storm cloud. The electrical energy turns into the heat and light energy of lightning and the sound energy of thunder.

Curiosity quiz

Look through the Physical science pages to identify each of the picture clues below.

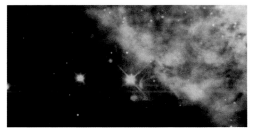
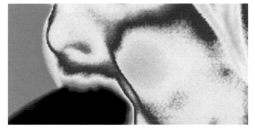

Become an expert...

on light, pages 82–83
on heat, pages 86–87

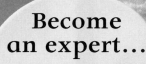

Energy cannot be destroyed. It turns into another form of energy when it's used.

Chain reactions

Changing energy from one type to another is called "energy conversion". The steps can be linked to make an energy chain.

Coal contains chemical energy.

Burning coal produces heat energy, which is used to boil water. Boiling water creates steam.

Moving steam is a form of kinetic (motion) energy, which operates turbines.

The kinetic energy produced by the moving turbines creates electricity.

Electrical energy used by television sets changes into light, sound, and heat energy.

Energy changes

All around you, energy is being converted from one form to another. You can make these changes happen yourself – just switch on a light to turn electrical energy into light energy.

Driving force
Car fuel is full of chemical energy. When the engine starts, the chemical energy is changed to heat energy. This is the first in a series of energy changes that make cars run.

Heat to sound
Some heat energy becomes sound energy. The roar of a racing-car engine can be deafening!

What name is given to energy sources like coal, oil, and gas?

Energy savings

Energy is precious, so people are finding extra ways to limit energy use.

 Roof insulation stops heat energy from escaping and helps keep houses warm.

 Energy-saving light bulbs last longer and use less energy than standard ones.

 Washing clothes at low temperatures saves the energy needed to heat water.

 Boiling only as much water as you need in the kettle saves time and energy.

Energy currents

Energy is transported through wires as currents of electricity. The electrical energy in this circuit comes from chemical energy in the battery.

Moving on

Some heat energy is changed to kinetic energy as the pistons move. The movement of the car is also kinetic energy.

Wheels of fire

Some of the kinetic energy in the wheels becomes heat energy. The hottest parts are shown white and yellow.

Become an expert...

on types of energy, pages **72–73**

on resources, pages **110–111**

Electricity

Have you ever thought about what powers your television, your computer, or the lights in your bedroom? A flow of electricity makes all these things work.

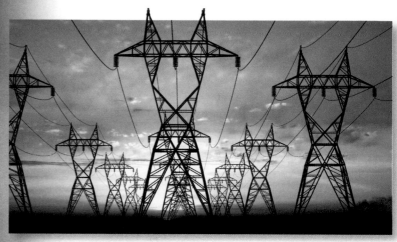

Power supply

Electricity travels to your home along wires above and sometimes below the ground. The wires above the ground hang on metal towers called pylons.

Making electricity

Electricity is a form of energy. It can be made using any source of energy, such as coal, gas, oil, wind, or sunlight. On a wind farm, wind turbines use the energy of moving air to create electricity.

Everyday electricity

We use electricity in all sorts of ways in our everyday lives.

Heating: electricity heats up household appliances such as irons and cookers.

Lighting: electricity lights up our homes, schools, offices, and streets.

Communication: electricity can power telephones and computers.

Transport: electricity is used to power certain vehicles, such as trams.

What's the name of a small object that can store electricity?

Circuits of power

An electric circuit is a loop that electricity can travel around. An electric current moves through the wires in this circuit, and lights up the bulb.

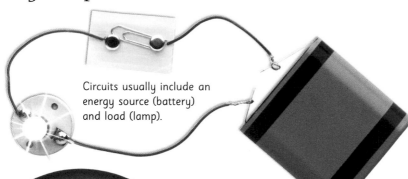

Circuits usually include an energy source (battery) and load (lamp).

Electrical cables

Electrical cables are made of metal and plastic. Electricity flows through the metal (which is called a conductor). The plastic (which is called an insulator) stops electricity escaping.

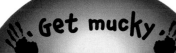

Get mucky

Rub a party balloon up and down on your clothes. The balloon will now stick to the wall. This is because rubbing it gives the balloon an electric charge.

Lightning strikes

When electricity builds up in one place it is called static electricity. A bolt of lightning is a huge spark of static electricity in the sky.

High voltage

Electricity can be very dangerous. This triangle is an international warning symbol. It means "Caution: risk of electric shock".

Food battery

Food that contains water and weak acid will conduct electricity. In a food battery, a chemical reaction between the metal and the acid in the food creates an electric current.

Magnetism

Magnets contain iron or a related metal. They exert a force called magnetism, which attracts objects with iron in them.

Magnets attract iron. This one has attracted a clump of steel paperclips because steel has an iron content.

Attract or repel?

When materials are pulled together, this force is called attraction. When materials push apart, it is called repulsion. Magnets can attract or repel each other.

Magnet rules

The ends of a magnet are called the north and south poles. Opposite poles attract each other. Similar poles repel each other.

Opposite poles of a magnet attract each other.

The Northern Lights are partly due to magnetic forces in our atmosphere.

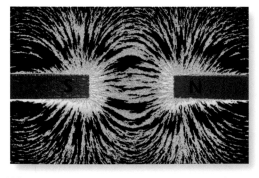

When opposite poles of a magnet face together, they attract. Iron filings show the lines of force between the two magnets.

Lights in the sky

Earth has a magnetic field.

Amazing lights are caused when particles in the solar wind (streaming from the Sun) are sucked into the atmosphere by Earth's magnetic field.

Earth as a magnet

Earth behaves as if there is a giant invisible magnet between the North and South poles. That's why we can use a compass to find our way.

What is a magnetometer?

Electromagnets

When an electric current flows through a wire coil, the coil becomes magnetic. This makes an electromagnet. Automatic doors, loudspeakers, and electric motors all use electromagnets.

Electromagnets are used in speakers.

Lifting with magnets

Some cranes use magnetic force, in the form of giant electromagnets, instead of hooks. The electromagnet can be switched on or off.

When switched on, the crane's electromagnet will attract huge pieces of iron and steel.

Magnetic rails

Maglev trains are held above a track by a magnetic force. Maglev is short for "magnetic levitation". The trains literally travel on air.

Maglev trains are being developed in Japan, and in Florida, USA.

Get mucky
Use a magnet to find out which things in your home are made from magnetic materials. Your magnet will be attracted to magnetic objects.

A device that measures the strength of a magnetic field.

Energy waves

If you throw a small pebble in a pond, the waves are small and close together. If you throw in a large rock, the waves are big and further apart. Just like water waves, energy travels in waves of different sizes.

● Radio waves

Radio waves have the longest wavelengths and are good at travelling far. Radio and TV programmes are broadcast as radio waves.

The spectrum

Light is a type of energy wave that we can see, but there are other types of energy wave that we can't see. Some have a longer wavelength than light, others have shorter waves.

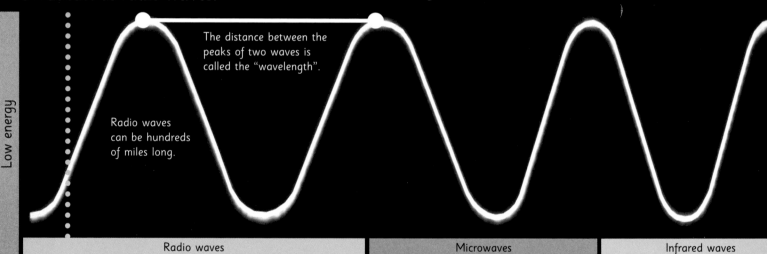

The distance between the peaks of two waves is called the "wavelength".

Low energy

Radio waves can be hundreds of miles long.

| Radio waves | Microwaves | Infrared waves |

● Microwaves

Microwaves are used to heat up food in microwave ovens. They are also used by mobile phones and by satellites in space.

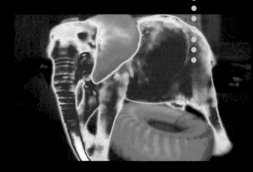

● Infrared waves

Hot objects give off invisible rays of heat called infrared waves. An infrared camera can detect these waves to create images.

What is invisible to human eyes but visible to the eyes of a bee?

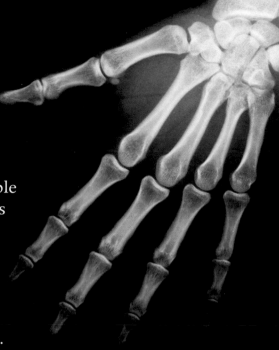

● Visible light
Light waves bounce off every object around us, allowing us to see things. Visible light includes all the colours of the rainbow, each of which has a particular wavelength.

● X-rays
X-rays are invisible waves that pass through soft parts of the body but not bone. This is why doctors can use X-rays to make images of bones.

High energy

| sible | UV rays | X-rays | Gamma rays |

● Gamma rays
The wavelengths of gamma rays can be as small as the nucleus of an atom. Gamma rays are packed with energy, which makes them powerful but deadly. They are used in hospitals to kill cancer cells.

● Ultraviolet (UV) light
As well as producing visible light, the Sun produces invisible rays of ultraviolet light. UV light makes you tan but too much of it can cause skin cancer and eye damage.

This man is being treated with gamma rays to kill cancer cells inside his body.

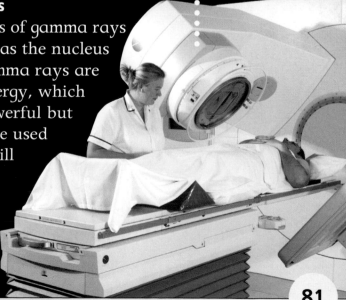

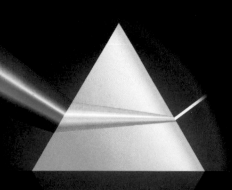

Light

Light is a form of energy that our eyes can detect. It comes in all the colours of the rainbow, but when the colours are mixed together, light is white.

Where does light come from?

Light comes from inside atoms. When an atom needs to lose energy, it spits out the energy as a particle of light.

The light of a flame is caused by a chemical reaction that releases energy stored in the burning wax.

Fireflies
Some animals create their own light. Fireflies have tails that flash a yellowish-green colour at night to attract mates.

Using light
We can use light for many different things.

CDs and DVDs store digital information that can be read by laser beam.

Cameras capture light in a split second to create photographs.

Telescopes magnify the light from distant stars and planets so we can see them.

Mirrors reflect light so we can see images of ourselves.

Periscopes bend light so we can see around corners.

Torches shine a beam of light to help us see in the dark.

Casting shadows
Light can only travel in straight lines. If something blocks its path, it casts a shadow – a dark area that the light cannot reach.

What's the fastest thing in the Universe?

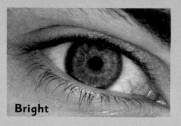
Bright

Dark

Light enters your eyes through your pupils (the black circles in the middle). Pupils can change size. When it's dark they get bigger to let more light in, and when it's bright they shrink so you don't get dazzled.

How your eye works

The human eye works like a camera. The front parts of the eye focus light rays just as a camera lens does. The focused rays form an upside-down image in the back of your eyeball.

Light beams
Unless it enters your eyes, light is invisible. The beam of light from a lighthouse can only be seen from the side if it catches mist or dust in the air, causing some of the light rays to bounce off towards you. Lighthouse beams sweep round in circles and can be seen from far out at sea.

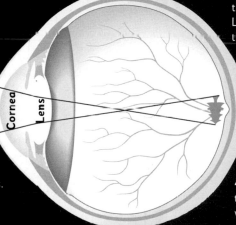

1. Light rays from the tree enter your eye.

Tree

Cornea

Lens

2. The cornea (front of eye) and lens focus the rays.

3. An image forms on the back of the eye. Light-sensing cells send the image to the brain.

4. The brain turns the image the right way up.

Reflecting light

When light hits a mirror, it bounces straight back off. If you look into a mirror, you see this bounced light as a reflection.

Convex mirrors bulge outwards. They make things look smaller but let you see a wider area.

Concave mirrors bulge inwards. They make things look bigger but show a smaller area.

83

Light. It travels at a thousand millions kph (620,000,000 mph).

Sound

Every sound starts with a vibration, like the quivering of a guitar string. The vibration squeezes and stretches the air between the vibrating object and your ear. This is a sound wave.

Get mucky

When you blow across a bottle, the air inside vibrates. Small air spaces vibrate more quickly than large spaces, making higher notes. So partly empty bottles produce lower notes than fuller ones.

Silent space

Sound can travel through solids, liquids, and gases, but it can't travel where there is no matter. There is no sound in space because there is no air.

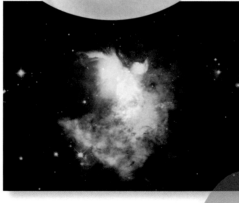

Sound waves travel through air like a wave along a coiled spring.

How hearing works

When a sound reaches your ears, it makes your eardrums vibrate. The vibrations are passed to your inner ear through tiny bones. From here, nerves send messages to your brain that allow you to recognize the sound.

Measuring sound

Loudness is measured in decibels.

 Rustling leaves make a sound of only 10 decibels.

 Whispering measures about 20 decibels.

 City traffic reaches approximately 85 decibels.

 Drums make a sound of around 105 decibels.

 Road-drills measure about 110 decibels.

 A lion's roar has been recorded at 114 decibels.

 Fireworks can measure 120 decibels or more.

 Jet engines sometimes hit 140 decibels.

Do all animals hear the same sounds?

Speeding sound

All sounds travel at the same speed, but they travel more quickly through solids and liquids than through gases. Supersonic jets fly faster than the speed of sound, so they can pass over you before you hear their sound.

When a supersonic jet breaks the speed of sound, it catches up with the sound waves in front of it and squashes them. As the air is squashed, it produces a sound called a "sonic boom".

The echo effect

Some animals use sound to communicate or to hunt. Dolphins "talk" by making clicks, barks and other sounds that other dolphins recognize. They also use clicks to find food – the sound bounces back off objects as an echo, so the dolphin can establish their shape and position. This is called

When sounds bounce back, the dolphin can tell if the object is a yummy fish or another dolphin!

No – dogs can hear higher notes than people, and squid can't hear at all.

Heat

Atoms and molecules are always jiggling about. The faster they move, the more energy an object has. We feel this energy as heat. When something is hot, its atoms are moving quickly. When something is cold, its atoms are moving slower.

Sources of heat

Heat can be produced in several different ways.

Friction (rubbing) makes heat. If you pull on a rope, your hands will feel warm.

Combustion means burning. When something burns, it produces heat.

Electricity is used to create heat in electric ovens and heaters.

Feel the heat

Heat always tries to spread from hot things to cooler things. When you touch a hot object, heat energy flows into your skin, triggering sense cells that make your skin feel hot. When you touch a cold object, heat flows out of your skin, triggering a different feeling.

Temperature

The temperature of an object tells you how hot it is on a numbered scale. A device called a thermometer is used to measure temperature.

Warm glow

Heat escapes from warm objects as invisible rays that travel like light. We call this infrared radiation. Special cameras use infrared rays rather than light to take photos. Hot areas appear white or red and cold areas are black.

Keep your cool

Heat travels from the Sun as infrared rays. Just like light, infrared rays are reflected away by white objects but absorbed by black objects. In hot countries, people paint houses white to reflect the heat and keep the indoors cool.

Can snow keep you warm?

Free ride

When land gets hot, it warms the air above it. The warm air rises. Birds use these areas of rising air (thermals) to lift them high in the sky.

Eagles can fly without flapping when they catch a thermal.

Conduction

Heat spreads through solids by a process called conduction. Hot atoms, which jiggle about a lot, knock into cooler atoms and make them jiggle faster, passing on the heat energy.

Heat is spreading along this metal bar. Metal is good at conducting heat quickly.

Convection

When air or water warms up, it rises, and cool air or water sinks to take its place. This process is called convection. Convection helps keep the ocean currents moving, spreading heat around the world.

weird or what?

Snakes called pit vipers have heat sensors on their heads. The heat sensors work like simple eyes, allowing the snakes to "see" the warmth of mice when hunting in the dark.

This satellite image shows the temperature of the world's oceans.

Keeping warm

Emperor penguins live in the icy Antarctic. Their feathers trap air, which stops too much heat escaping from their body by conduction. This trapping layer is called insulation.

Yes, if you use it to build an igloo. Snow is a good insulator.

Forces

A force is simply a push or a pull. When you push or pull something to make it move, you are using forces. Some forces work only when objects are touching, but others, such as gravity and magnetism, work at a distance.

Gravity

The force that makes things fall to the ground is gravity. Gravity keeps Earth in orbit around the Sun and keeps the Moon in orbit around Earth. It is one of the most important forces in the Universe.

This space shuttle needs three rockets to help it escape from Earth's gravitational pull.

If the chains broke, the riders would shoot off in a straight line.

Lift-off

A huge force is needed to make a spacecraft take off and escape Earth's gravity. A force called thrust is provided by rockets. The rockets make hot gases, which expand and stream out at the bottom to push the spacecraft up into the air at great speed.

In a spin

On a merry-go-round, the riders feel they're being pushed outwards. This pushing, called centrifugal force, isn't a real force. It's caused by the riders' bodies trying to move in a straight line while the chains are holding them back.

What force makes compass needles point towards the North Pole?

Get mucky

Rub your hands together as hard and fast as you can for ten seconds and see how hot they get. The heat is caused by the force of friction acting on your skin.

Friction

When objects rub or slide against each other, they create a force called friction. Friction slows down moving objects and wastes their energy, turning the energy into heat.

To reduce friction, the bottom surface of these skis is very smooth and coated with slippery wax.

Friction slows a skier down.

Electric forces

When objects become charged with electricity, they pull on each other with an invisible force a bit like magnetism. If you rub a balloon on your hair, the balloon becomes charged and will stick to your shirt.

Buoyancy

What makes objects float? The answer is a force called buoyancy. If an object is lighter than water, the force of buoyancy outweighs gravity and the object floats.

Gravity pulls the duck down.

Upthrust from the water keeps the duck afloat.

Forces and motion

It can be difficult to make an object move, but once it is moving, it will go on moving until something stops it. Force is needed to start something moving, make it move faster, and make it stop.

The football would stay still if the footballer didn't kick it.

Newton's laws of motion

In 1687, Sir Isaac Newton worked out three important rules that explain how forces make things move. They have become the foundation of physics and work for just about everything, from footballs to frogs.

Newton's first law
An object stays still if it isn't being pushed or pulled by a force, or it keeps moving in a straight line at a constant speed.

Forces make things accelerate. The force is created by the cyclist's powerful legs.

Newton's second law
The bigger the force and the lighter the object, the greater the acceleration. A professional cyclist with a lightweight bike will accelerate faster than a normal person cycling to work.

Newton's third law
Every action has an equal and opposite reaction. The leaf moves away as the frog leaps in the opposite direction.

How fast will a skydiver fall?

Speed and velocity

Speed is different to velocity. How quick you are going is easy to work out – divide how far you travel by the time it takes. Your velocity is how fast you travel in a particular direction. Changing direction without slowing reduces your velocity, but your speed stays the same.

If you drive 80 km (50 miles) in two hours, your speed is 40 kph (25 mph).

Accelerating is fun, but in science it can be confusing. This is because acceleration doesn't just mean speeding up. It is any change in velocity. So it is also used to describe slowing down and changing direction.

The golf ball will carry on rolling until friction, gravity, and air resistance slow it down.

Inertia

When things are standing still or moving, they are quite happy to continue with what they are doing. This stubbornness is called inertia – it is the object's resistance to change.

Become an expert...

on magnetism, pages **78–79**

on gravity, pages **88–89**

Balanced forces

Forces act on objects all the time. Opposing forces can be balanced out. When this happens the object won't be pushed in any direction.

Rescue helicopters balance forces so they can hover above the waves.

LIFT

DRAG/ FRICTION

THRUST

GRAVITY

The maximum velocity of falling through air is 200 kph (124 mph).

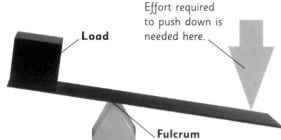

Effort required to push down is needed here.

Load

Fulcrum

Levers

A lever is a bar that swivels on a fixed point or fulcrum and makes it easier to move a load. When you move your end further (the effort), the load at the other end moves a short way powerfully.

One type of lever works like a see-saw with the fulcrum between the load and the effort.

Another type places the load between the fulcrum and the effort (as on a wheelbarrow).

A third type of lever, shown by tongs, places the effort between the fulcrum and the load.

Machines

Machines make tasks easier. They reduce the effort you need to move something, or the time it takes. They work either by spreading the load, or by concentrating your efforts.

Axle

Wheel and axle

An axle goes through the centre of a wheel. Together they work as a simple rotating machine that makes it easier to move something from one place to another.

Gears

Gears are wheels with teeth that interlock so that one wheel turns another. They increase speed or force. Gears on a bicycle affect how much you must turn the pedal to spin the wheel.

The pedal turns a wheel, which turns a smaller wheel at a greater speed.

Get mucky

Try walking straight up a hill and then zig-zag your way up. The winding path works like a simple machine. It increases the distance you walk, but decreases the effort you use.

Name six simple machines.

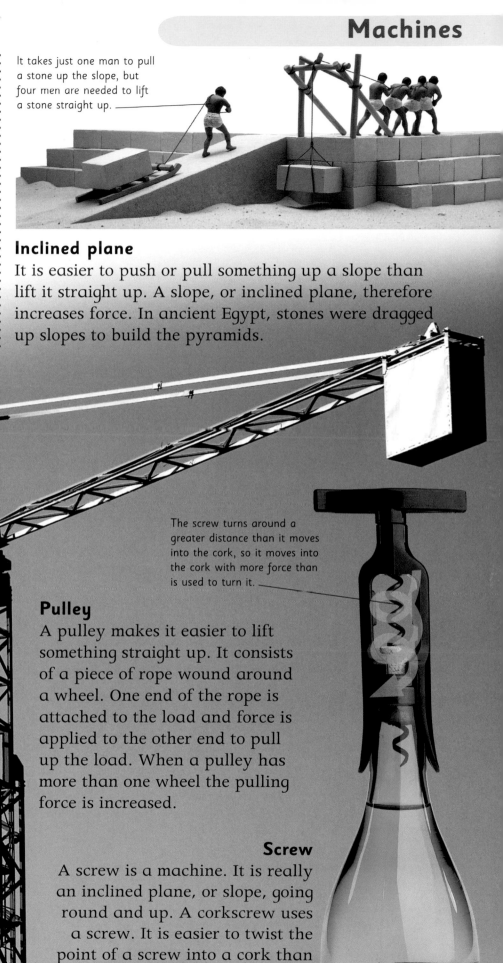

Wedge

An axe blade is an efficient but simple machine that increases force. When it hits the wood, the wedge forces the wood to split apart between its fibres.

It takes just one man to pull a stone up the slope, but four men are needed to lift a stone straight up.

Inclined plane

It is easier to push or pull something up a slope than lift it straight up. A slope, or inclined plane, therefore increases force. In ancient Egypt, stones were dragged up slopes to build the pyramids.

The screw turns around a greater distance than it moves into the cork, so it moves into the cork with more force than is used to turn it.

The crane lifts up heavy loads with a system of pulleys.

Pulley

A pulley makes it easier to lift something straight up. It consists of a piece of rope wound around a wheel. One end of the rope is attached to the load and force is applied to the other end to pull up the load. When a pulley has more than one wheel the pulling force is increased.

Screw

A screw is a machine. It is really an inclined plane, or slope, going round and up. A corkscrew uses a screw. It is easier to twist the point of a screw into a cork than to push a spike straight in.

Lever, wheel and axle, gear, wedge, inclined plane, and pulley.

The Universe

The Universe is everything that exists. It includes Earth, the Sun, and the other stars in our galaxy. Beyond our galaxy are countless other galaxies. The Universe was created in the "Big Bang", around 13.7 billion years ago.

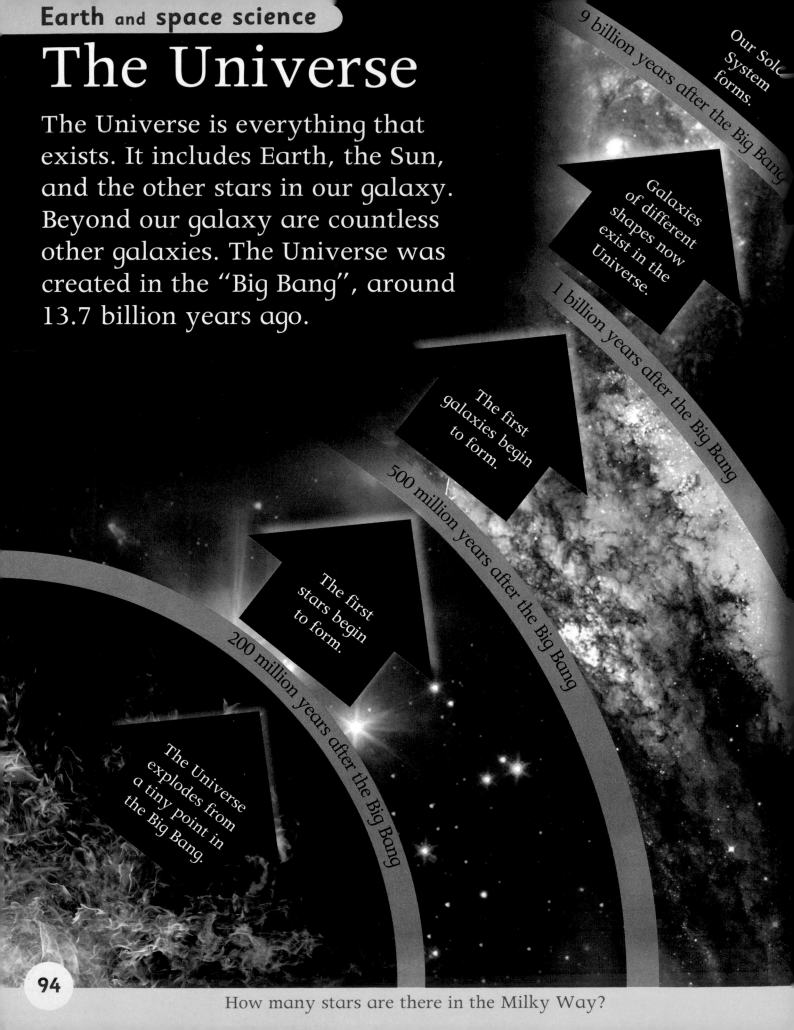

9 billion years after the Big Bang

Our Solar System forms.

Galaxies of different shapes now exist in the Universe.

1 billion years after the Big Bang

The first galaxies begin to form.

500 million years after the Big Bang

The first stars begin to form.

200 million years after the Big Bang

The Universe explodes from a tiny point in the Big Bang.

How many stars are there in the Milky Way?

Galaxies

Galaxies are groups of stars held together by gravity. There are more than 100,000 million stars in a typical galaxy. Galaxies are different shapes. Some are spirals and some are oval.

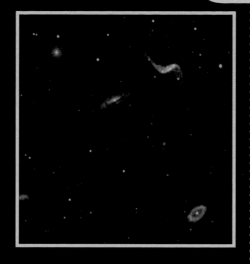

Near neighbour

The nearest galaxy to our own is the spiral-shaped Andromeda galaxy. It would take around 2.2 million years to get there – if you were travelling at the speed of light!

The Milky Way

Our Solar System is part of a galaxy called the Milky Way. From the inside (where we are), it looks like a haze of light in the sky.

Curiosity quiz

Look through the Earth and space science pages. Can you identify the picture clues below?

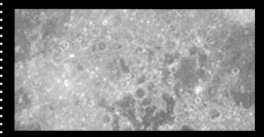

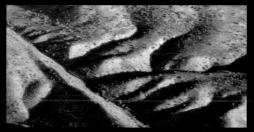

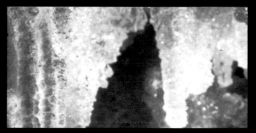

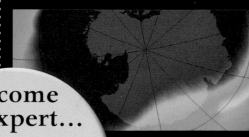

Become an expert...

on how stars form, pages 96–97
on the Solar System, pages 98–99

Between 200 billion and 400 billion.

Starry skies

There are many more stars in the Universe than there are grains of sand on all the beaches on Earth. Many are far brighter than our Sun.

The lives of stars

The lives of stars begin inside thick clouds of gas in space called nebulae.

Supernovae
The most massive stars end their lives in huge supernovae explosions.

White dwarfs
The outer layers of the star are eventually thrown off into space. The cooling core is left behind. This is called a white dwarf. White dwarfs are no bigger than Earth.

Red giants
Stars are fuelled by the gas hydrogen. They burn until the hydrogen starts to run out. Then they expand, forming a red giant star.

Nebulae
Gravity pulls together little knots of dust and gas inside the nebulae. Each one could become a star, as gravity squeezes it tighter and it becomes hotter.

Stars in motion

The position of the stars seems to change throughout the night. The stars are not really moving, though. It is the Earth that is turning beneath them.

How many stars can you see on a clear, dark night?

Remnants
The fragments of the star can remain glowing in space for hundreds of years.

The Sun is made mostly of hydrogen.

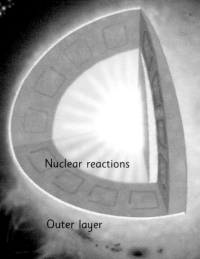

Nuclear reactions

Outer layer

Starshine

Our Sun is a star that is halfway through its life. In the life cycle it would sit between being formed within a nebula and becoming a red giant.

Black holes

When the biggest stars explode, most material is blown outwards. But the core is crushed and collapses to form a black hole.

Shapes in the sky

Constellations are groups of stars that can be seen from Earth. They all have names – often related to their shapes. This is the Plough, in Ursa Major.

Our Solar System

The Solar System is our own small part of space. It is made up of the Sun, eight planets, and countless smaller objects like comets.

Family of worlds

The planets all move around the Sun in paths called orbits. They are held in these orbits by gravity.

Neptune is the furthest planet from the Sun in the Solar System.

Uranus has 13 rings and 27 moons.

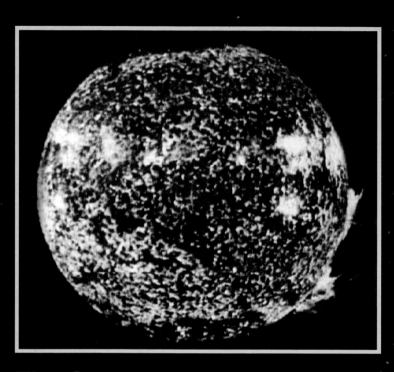

Mars is red because the soil on its surface is full of rust.

Jupiter is the largest planet in the Solar System. It has more than 60 moons.

The Sun

The Sun is our closest star. All the heat and light we need to survive on Earth comes from it. Although the Sun is about half way through its life, it will continue to burn for another five billion years.

How old is the Solar System?

Days and years

All planets spin. The time each one takes to spin once is called a day. The time taken for a planet to go all the way round the Sun is a year. Days and years are different lengths on different planets.

Saturn has rings made of ice, dust, and rock.

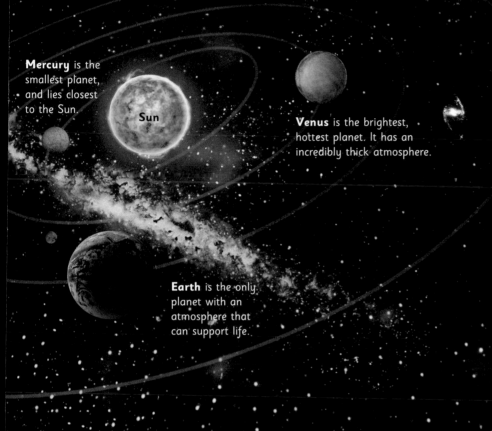

Mercury is the smallest planet, and lies closest to the Sun.

Sun

Venus is the brightest, hottest planet. It has an incredibly thick atmosphere.

Earth is the only planet with an atmosphere that can support life.

Fire in the sky

There are many other objects in space. Comets are chunks of ice, rock, and dust. Meteors are lumps of rock that burn up as they enter Earth's atmosphere. We see them as shooting stars.

Neptune Uranus Saturn Jupiter Mars Venus Earth Mercury Sun

How big?

All the planets are tiny in comparison with the Sun, but the outer planets are much bigger than the four closest to it. The Sun is 100 times wider than Earth!

About 4.6 billion years old.

99

The Moon

Our Moon is a cold, dusty world that moves around the Earth in space. There is no air or water on the Moon, so nothing can live there. Scientists think that the Moon is around 4.5 billion years old.

As well as craters, there are mountains and valleys on the Moon's surface.

Battered surface

The surface of the Moon is covered in craters. These have been caused by meteors crashing into it over millions of years.

From Earth, we only see the near side of the Moon.

The far side
The Moon takes the same time to turn all the way round as it does to go around the Earth. This means we always see the same side of it. The far side of the Moon can only be seen by spacecraft.

Ocean bulges
The pull of gravity between the Moon and the Earth tugs on the Earth's oceans, making them bulge on either side of the planet. As the Moon spins round Earth, the bulges move. The sea rises and falls in tides.

Orbiting Moon
The Moon moves round the Earth once every 27 days. As the Moon, Sun, and Earth move, we see different amounts of the Moon lit by the Sun each night. These different views are called "phases".

Between the bulges of water, the sea falls and it is low tide.

As each bulge arrives, the sea rises and it is high tide.

How far is the Moon from Earth?

Moon men

The Moon is the only alien world that humans have visited. In 1969, astronauts walked on the Moon for the first time.

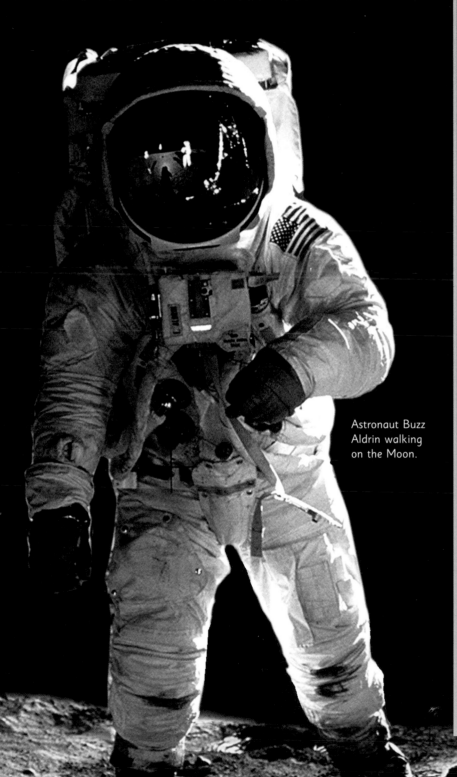

Astronaut Buzz Aldrin walking on the Moon.

Lunar eclipse

When the Earth passes exactly between the Moon and the Sun, the Earth's shadow falls on the Moon and blocks out most of its light. This is called a lunar eclipse.

Solar eclipse

When the Moon passes exactly between the Earth and the Sun, its shadow falls on some parts of the Earth. This is a solar eclipse.

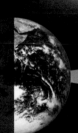

Sunlight

Total eclipse

People at the centre of the Moon's shadow experience a total solar eclipse. In other places, only part of the light is blocked.

Around 384,000 km (239,000 miles).

Earth's structure

Earth is the only planet in the Solar System that can support life, because it's just the right distance from the Sun. Our amazing world is a huge ball of liquid rock with a solid surface.

Seen from space, Earth is a mass of blue oceans and swirling clouds.

Crust

Core

Outer core

Mantle

Inside the Earth

If you could cut the Earth open, you'd see it's made up of layers. The thin top layer, where we live, is called the crust. Underneath is a layer of syrup-like rock called the mantle, then an outer core of molten (liquid) iron and nickel. At the centre is a solid iron-and-nickel core.

Life-support systems

Earth's atmosphere and its surface water play an important role in supporting life. They help keep our planet at just the right temperature by absorbing the Sun's heat and moving it around the world.

What is the biggest ocean on Earth?

Volcanoes

Volcanoes are openings in the Earth's crust. Sometimes magma (melted rock) from just beneath the crust bursts through these openings as a volcanic eruption. Lots of ash and dust shoot out too.

Making mountains

The Himalayas started to form 50 million years ago, when two moving plates collided. The mountains are still growing!

Earthquakes often occur along the San Andreas Fault.

Fault lines

Earthquakes happen when continents rub against each other.

Drifting continents

The world hasn't always looked like it does now. Millions of years ago, all the land was joined together. Slowly, it broke up and the continents drifted apart.

Cracked crust

Earth's top layer is made up of giant pieces called "plates". These fit together a bit like a jigsaw, but they're constantly moving. Volcanoes and earthquakes often happen in the weak spots where plates move against each other.

| 200 million years ago | 135 million years ago | 10 million years ago |

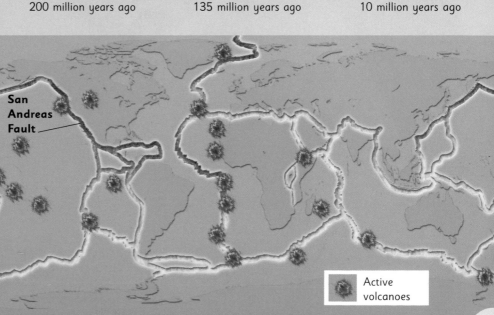

San Andreas Fault

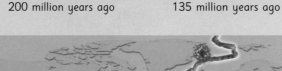
Active volcanoes

Rocks and minerals

The Earth's crust is made up of different rocks. Some of these are hard but others are soft and crumbly. They are formed in different ways.

Serpentine is a mineral that stone carvers use to create works of art.

Gabbro is a rock that is used to make kitchen surfaces and floors.

White mica is a mineral that you can find in some kinds of toothpaste.

What is a rock?

A rock is formed from minerals. Most rocks are made up of different minerals, but some contain just one. There are three main types of rock: igneous, sedimentary, and metamorphic.

Fossils in stones
Fossils are the remains or imprints of plants and animals that died millions of years ago, preserved in stone.

The rock cycle

Over many years, the rocks in Earth's crust gradually change from one type into another. They are transformed by wind, water, pressure, and heat.

Igneous rock
Igneous rocks are made when hot molten magma from the Earth's interior cools and solidifies. Some hardens underground like granite. Some erupts first as lava in a volcano.

Sedimentary rock
Wind and water wear rocks away. Small pieces wash into the sea. These settle into layers, which pack together to form sedimentary rocks, such as limestone and sandstone.

Metamorphic rock
Sometimes rocks are crushed underground, or scorched by hot magma. Then they may be transformed into new rocks such as marble, slate, and gneiss.

Which type of rock floats on water?

What is a mineral?

A mineral is a solid that occurs naturally. It is made up of chemicals and has a crystal structure. Minerals are everywhere you look. We use minerals to build cars and computers, fertilize soil, and to clean our teeth.

Rock salt is a mineral that is spread on roads in icy weather. It makes the ice melt.

Mineral mixtures

Granite rock is made up of different coloured minerals. The black mineral is mica, the pink is feldspar, and the grey mineral is quartz.

Feldspar is used for glazing ceramics.

Mica is ground up and used in paint.

Quartz can also occur as the gemstone amethyst.

Crystals

Minerals usually form crystals. Crystals have a number of flat surfaces. The largest crystals form when minerals in magma or trapped liquids cool very slowly.

Quartz stalactites form in caves over thousands of years.

Minerals in your home

Halite Salt is the mineral halite. We add it to our food for flavour.

Quartz from sand is used to make the silicon chips in calculators and computers.

Kaolinite is used to make crockery. It is also used to make paper look glossy.

Illite is a clay mineral and is used in terracotta pots and bricks.

Mica is used to make glittery paint and nail polish.

Graphite is the 'lead' in pencils. It is also used in bicycle brakes.

Rhodochrosite is a rose-coloured gemstone used in jewellery.

Pumice is filled with air bubbles, so some pieces can float.

Shaping the land

The surface of our planet never stops changing. Over millions of years, land is slowly worn away by wind, rain, and rivers. Floods, volcanoes, and earthquakes can change the shape of the land in just a few hours.

River power
The Grand Canyon formed over millions of years as the Colorado River slowly wore ever deeper into the rock.

Going underground
Caves form when rain seeps underground and eats away at soft rock such as limestone.

Coastal shapes

Powerful waves shape the coastlines around the world's oceans.

 Bays form where waves wear into areas of softer rock along the coast.

 Headlands are areas of harder rock that have not been worn away.

 Sea arches form when waves open up cracks in headlands.

 Sea stacks are pillars of rock left in the sea after an arch collapses.

Glaciers at work
Glaciers are huge rivers of ice that flow slowly off snowcapped mountains. Broken rock sticks to the bottom of the glacier, which then wears away the land like sandpaper, carving out a deep, U-shaped valley.

What is the most active volcano on Earth?

New islands

Some volcanoes are hidden under the sea. When they erupt, they can give birth to whole new islands, like Surtsey in Iceland (left). Surtsey burst out of the sea in 1963.

Before flood   After flood

Floods

Heavy rain makes rivers overflow, causing floods. Floods have enormous power and can wreck buildings and re-shape the land.

Hills of sand

In deserts, winds blow sand into hills called dunes. In some deserts the dunes stretch for hundreds of miles, forming a "sand sea".

Worn by wind

Strong winds can lift sand off the ground and blast it hard against rocks. The rock is worn into strange shapes.

Mount Kilauea in Hawaii.

Soil

Soil is the thin layer of loose material on the land. Soil contains minerals, air, water, and decaying organic matter.

Layers in soil

Soil builds up in layers over many years. Plant roots grow in the topsoil, which is generally the richest in plant food. The lower layers are rocky. Plant roots do not reach this far down in the soil.

Humus

Topsoil

Subsoil

Regolith

Bedrock

Healthy humus

Humus is a dark, rich substance made up of rotting plants and animals (called "organic matter"). It contains lots of nutrients, which plants need to grow.

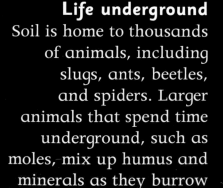

Life underground

Soil is home to thousands of animals, including slugs, ants, beetles, and spiders. Larger animals that spend time underground, such as moles, mix up humus and minerals as they burrow through the soil.

What is a scientist who studies soil called?

Sizing up soil

Different types of soil have different sized particles.

Sandy soils contain particles about 2 mm (0.08 in) across.

Clay soils have very small particles. Water collects between them.

Loamy soils have a mixture of small and large particles.

Soil erosion

When soil is farmed too much, its nutrients get used up. The topsoil blows or washes away. Not many plants can survive in these areas without the rich topsoil.

Ploughing helps keep soil fertile.

Ploughing breaks up soil, to stop it getting hard and solid. This helps crops grow more easily.

FORD 7740

Important earthworms

Earthworms help to make fertile soil. Their burrows let air into the soil, and create pathways for water to move around more easily. Earthworms also help the remains of plants and animals to decompose. This releases important nutrients into the soil. Earthworm waste is good for soil too!

Get mucky

Half fill a jar with soil and top it up with water. Put on the lid and shake. Leave for a day. The soil should separate into layers.

A pedologist.

Earth and space science

Resources in the ground

The ground holds many useful things, from fuels like coal and oil, to drinking water, and building materials. These valuable items are known as resources and we have dug, drilled, and searched for them for many years.

Sea level   **Rig**

People drill holes to extract oil and gas from deep under the sea floor.

Finding fuels

Oil and gas are often found in pockets deep underground. Sometimes, these are even below the seabed. Coal develops closer to the surface in layers called seams.

Deep drilling
Oil rigs far out at sea use huge drills to extract the liquid oil from the ground. Coal is solid and is dug out in mines or pits.

In hot water

Water in the ground can get very hot near volcanoes. In Iceland, they use this naturally hot water to heat houses or make steam to turn electricity generators.

Which underground resource are plastics made from?

Getting gas

Gas is only found in certain places. To get it to where it is needed, it is fed through very long pipes, or changed into liquid and put in special ships.

Making glass

Glass is made by melting together sand, soda ash, and ground limestone. People blow or machine press the red-hot mineral mixture into different shapes that set hard and clear as the glass cools.

Glass bottles are shaped from molten glass.

Extracting metals

Most metals are found underground as minerals in rocks called ores. Giant machines dig up the ore. The metal is extracted, or taken out, from the ore using heat.

Metal variety

Different metal resources have different uses.

Aluminium is a soft metal used to make cans, aircraft, and car bodies.

Gold is rare and looks attractive, so it is often used to make jewellery.

Iron is strong. It is used to make steel for ships, buildings, and pylons.

Copper conducts electricity and is used to make electrical wires.

Creating concrete

Concrete is an important building material. It is a mixture of sand, gravel, cement, and water. All these ingredients are found in the ground.

Fresh and salt water

Earth is often called the blue planet because 75 per cent of its surface is covered in water. Most of the Earth's water is salt water in the oceans. Less than one per cent of all the water on Earth is fresh.

Freshwater sources

People get fresh water from different sources on Earth's surface, including rivers, streams, lakes, and reservoirs.

Rivers and streams flow from mountains down to the oceans.

Lakes are natural dips in the Earth where water collects.

Reservoirs are man-made lakes that are built to store water.

The hydrosphere

The hydrosphere is the name for all the water on Earth. It includes oceans, rivers, and lakes. It also includes water that is frozen, such as icebergs.

Trapped in ice

Less than 33 per cent of fresh water is usable by humans. The rest is frozen in glaciers or icebergs (below), or as huge sheets of ice at the North and South poles.

Water for life

All animals – and most other living things – must have water to survive. In mammals, including humans, water is part of the blood and of organs such as the skin and brain. There is water in every cell in your body!

How much of your body is water?

Salty seas

The world's oceans are salty because they contain a lot of dissolved chemicals that scientists call salts. Drinking water also contains salts, but only in small amounts, so you can't taste them.

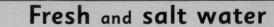

The Dead Sea contains so much salt that people can just float on the surface.

Surviving in salt water

Countless animals live in water. They don't drink, but take water into their bodies in other ways. Fish often absorb water as it washes in and out of their gills. Salt-water fish absorb only a little of the salt.

Get mucky

Put an egg in a glass of water. The egg will sink. Start stirring in salt until the egg rises. The egg will eventually float because salt water is denser than fresh water.

Estuary life

An estuary is the wide part of a river where it nears the sea. When the tide comes in, salt water flows into the estuary. When the tide goes out, the estuary contains mostly fresh water from the river or stream that flows into it. Mangrove trees like these are able to live in the changing estuary water.

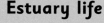
Your body is approximately 66 per cent water.

The water cycle

Water is constantly on the move, between oceans, land, air, and rivers. This movement is called the water cycle.

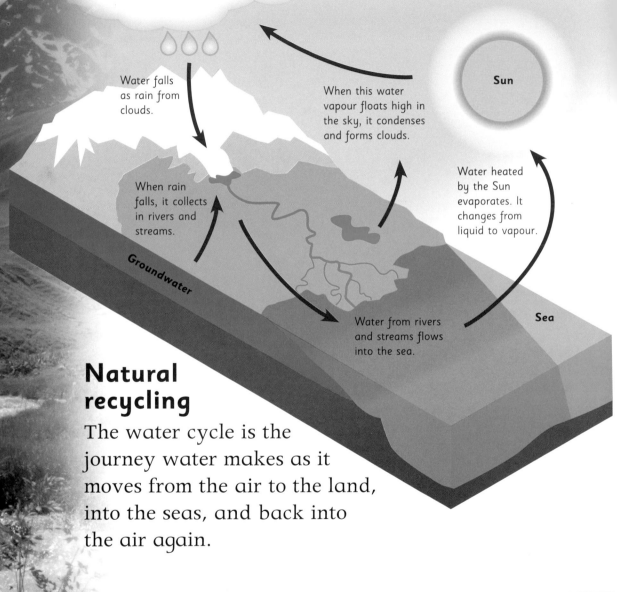

Water falls as rain from clouds.

When this water vapour floats high in the sky, it condenses and forms clouds.

Sun

Water heated by the Sun evaporates. It changes from liquid to vapour.

When rain falls, it collects in rivers and streams.

Groundwater

Water from rivers and streams flows into the sea.

Sea

Natural recycling

The water cycle is the journey water makes as it moves from the air to the land, into the seas, and back into the air again.

On the dry side

Moisture-laden sea air has to rise when it hits a coastal mountain. Since air cools as it rises, all the moisture condenses into rain. So, on the other side of the mountain, no rain falls – this area is called a rainshadow.

What is electricity generated by running water called?

Groundwater

In the water cycle, some water seeps underground, where it collects in rocks and sometimes forms pools in caves. Some groundwater is pumped up and used for drinking or irrigation.

Using water

Fresh water is trapped in reservoirs and then piped to homes, businesses, and farms. When you turn on a tap, the water that comes out has been on a long journey!

Damp ground

Wetlands form on land in areas where fresh water does not drain away. They provide a home for many water-loving plants, birds, animals, and fish.

Saving water

There is a limited amount of fresh water on Earth. If we want to make sure there's enough to go around, it's important that everyone uses less.

Turn off taps when you finish brushing your teeth or washing.

Flush the toilet only when necessary. Some toilets have two flush controls.

Don't run the dishwasher when it's half empty – wait until it's full.

Take a shower instead of a bath. Showering uses much less water.

Drought

When very little rain falls, experts call this a drought. Droughts do not occur only in deserts – any area that gets much less rain than usual is said to be suffering from drought.

Hydroelectricity.

The atmosphere

Planet Earth is wrapped in a thin layer of air called the atmosphere. Without this protective blanket of gases, life on Earth could not exist.

Gases in air

Air is a mixture of different gases, including nitrogen, oxygen, and carbon dioxide. Oxygen is vital for plants and animals as it allows them to breathe. Carbon dioxide is vital for plants. They absorb it from the air and use the carbon atoms to help build new leaves and stems.

Shimmering particles
The atmosphere is mainly made up of gases, but it also contains tiny particles of dust, pollen, and water droplets. All particles can cause a haze in the air when the Sun shines through them.

The greenhouse effect
If there was no atmosphere, the Sun's warming rays would bounce off Earth and disappear into space. But the atmosphere traps some of the heat, making Earth warm enough for us to survive.

From space, the atmosphere looks like a blue haze over Earth.

Protective layer
A gas called ozone in the atmosphere protects Earth from harmful rays in sunlight. Above Antarctica there is an area of the ozone layer that is much thinner than anywhere else. This "ozone hole" was caused by chemical pollution.

How far up from the ground does space officially begin?

Into thin air

Like everything else, air is pulled by gravity. Most air molecules are pulled close to the ground, where the air is thick and easy to breathe. Higher up, air is so thin that climbers need oxygen tanks.

Layers of the atmosphere

The atmosphere is made up of layers, each with a different name. The bottom layer is the troposphere, where clouds form and planes fly. Above this, the air gets thinner and thinner as the atmosphere merges into space.

Light spectacular

Sunlight can create dazzling effects as it strikes the atmosphere and is scattered by air, water, and dust.

 Rainbows form when water droplets reflect sunlight and split it into different colours.

 The sky looks blue on clear days because air molecules scatter blue light the most.

 At sunset and sunrise, dust and hazy cloud in the air turn the sky orange and red.

Moving water

The atmosphere is always swirling around, creating winds. The winds push on the oceans, causing the water to swirl too. These swirling currents carry warmth around the planet.

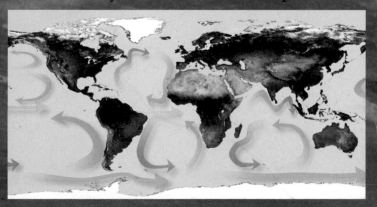

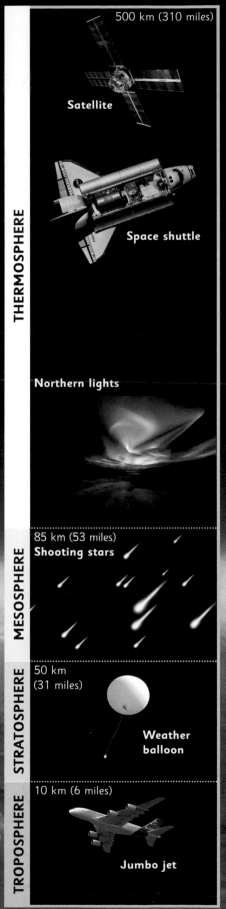

THERMOSPHERE

500 km (310 miles)

Satellite

Space shuttle

Northern lights

85 km (53 miles)
Shooting stars

MESOSPHERE

50 km (31 miles)

STRATOSPHERE

Weather balloon

10 km (6 miles)

TROPOSPHERE

Jumbo jet

Weather

Is it sunny or rainy? Is there snow on the ground or a thunderstorm brewing? People are always interested in the weather because it affects what we do and what we wear.

Kites stay high in the air by catching the wind.

Weather words

Here are some main features of the weather.

 Sunshine gives us heat and light. It warms the air and dries the land.

 Clouds are made from tiny water droplets. Dark clouds mean rain is coming.

 Hailstones are balls of ice that grow inside thunderclouds.

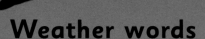 **Wind** is air moving around. Winds can be a light breeze or a strong gale.

 Rain is drops of water that fall from clouds. Rain is very good for plant life.

 Snow is made from tiny bits of ice. It falls instead of rain when it is very cold.

Predicting the weather

Weather forecasters look at pictures beamed back from weather satellites. Computers then help forecasters work out what the weather is going to be like over the next few days.

Rainy days

Rain clouds form when warm, moist air rises upwards and then cools. Droplets of water join together until they become so heavy that they fall. Rain clouds look dark because sunlight cannot shine through the droplets.

Which is bigger: a tornado or a hurricane?

Wildfires

Long periods of hot or dry weather can make plants dry out so much that they catch fire easily when struck by lightning. This can lead to a raging wildfire that burns down whole forests.

Stormy weather

Lightning strikes when electricity builds up in clouds. The electricity is created when ice crystals in the clouds rub against each other. A bolt of lightning heats the air around it so quickly that the air explodes, creating the rumbling noise we call thunder.

The brightest bolts of lightning travel upwards from the ground to the clouds.

Winds on the move

Wind is moving air. Warm air rises and cool air sinks. This movement is what makes the wind blow.

Twisters

Tornadoes (twisters) are whirling funnels of wind that form beneath massive thunderclouds. The fierce wind can do enormous damage, and the funnel can suck up debris like a gigantic vacuum cleaner.

weird or what?

Hailstones can grow to be enormous in certain conditions. The biggest hailstone weighed 1 kg (2 lb) and was over 40 cm (16 in) across!

A hurricane is thousands of times bigger than a tornado.

The energy crisis

People around the world use energy for many different purposes – from powering cars, to heating homes. Most of this energy comes from burning coal, oil and natural gas (fossil fuels). But these fuels won't last forever, and their fumes are damaging the atmosphere.

Nuclear power stations generate energy by splitting atoms.

Global warming

Burning fossil fuels fills the air with greenhouse gases, which trap some of the Sun's heat in the atmosphere. If Earth becomes too warm, the icebergs will melt, the sea level will rise, and deserts will spread.

Alternative energy

We need to find sources of energy other than fossil fuels – sources which cause less pollution and will not run out. Nuclear power is one option. Others possibilities include energy from sunlight, wind, and waves.

Heat from the Sun enters through the atmosphere.

Greenhouse gases trap heat, although some escapes back into the atmosphere.

The wind provides a limitless supply of non-polluting energy. However, wind turbines are large and can be costly to set up.

What are fossil fuels made of?

Cleaner cars

Ordinary petrol cars use a lot of oil, and produce harmful fumes. Now car makers are looking for alternatives to petrol. Electric cars do not give off any kind of fumes. Hydrogen engines burn hydrogen gas, and only give off water.

To recharge an electric car, you just plug it in.

Rising energy needs

As the world's population grows, we are using more and more energy. But to stop global warming, we may have to reduce the amount of energy we all use.

Energy-saving homes

This house saves energy by using solar panels and wind turbines to generate its own non-polluting electricity. The walls are thick, so that less energy is needed to heat the house.

To reduce the energy used in manufacturing, it's a good idea to use recycled building materials.

Making a difference

There are lots of small things we can all do to save energy.

 Start growing your own vegetables and fruit, even if they're only in pots.

 When planning a holiday, remember that trains, boats, and cars use less energy than aeroplanes.

 Instead of buying new clothes, swap with a friend or buy them second-hand.

 Eat local food that hasn't travelled miles, because transporting food costs energy.

 Don't throw away glass, plastics, metal, or paper – reuse or recycle them.

 Take your own bags when you go shopping. Making plastic bags takes energy.

 Don't leave your TV or DVD on standby – this wastes lots of electricity.

 Hang your laundry outside to dry. Don't waste electricity running a dryer.

 Ask your parents about insulating the roof to prevent heat from escaping.

 If you get cold, put on a jumper instead of turning up your heating.

The remains of plants and animals that lived millions of years ago.

Glossary

attraction The force that pushes things together. The opposite ends ("poles") of two magnets attract each other.

bacteria Tiny one-celled creatures found all around us. Some bacteria are good, but others cause disease.

biofuel Fuel made from the remains of living things. Wood and biogas made from animal droppings are both biofuels.

carbohydrate Along with fats and proteins, energy-rich carbohydrates like sugar and starch are one of the three major food groups.

carnivore An animal that eats only meat. Lions, wolves, sharks, and crocodiles are carnivores.

carrion The remains of dead animals that other animals eat.

chlorophyll The pigment in plants that gives them their green colour.

circuit A loop that an electric current travels around.

compound A chemical made when two or more elements are joined by a chemical reaction.

continent One of Earth's huge land masses, like Asia. There are seven continents.

electromagnet A powerful magnet created by a flow of electricity through a coil.

endorphins Brain chemicals that make you feel happy and reduce pain.

erosion Wearing away by wind or water.

estuary The wide part of a river where it meets the sea.

fertilization A process in which the male and female parts of an animal or plant join together to reproduce.

force A push or a pull. Gravity is the force that keeps you on the ground.

fossil fuels Fuels that come from the earth and are the remains of living things. Coal, oil, and gas are all fossil fuels.

genes Tiny chemical units holding the information that makes you who you are.

global warming The slow rise in average temperatures around the world.

habitat The place where a group of animals and plants live, such as a desert or park.

herbivore An animal that eats only plants. Cows, koalas, and elephants are herbivores.

invertebrates Animals that don't have a backbone.

laboratory A place where scientists carry out their experiments.

limestone Rock made from animal shells built up in layers over thousands of years.

What word means the natural world all around us?

migration The movement of animals, particularly birds, from one place to another to find food or warmth.

mixture Two or more combined substances that are not joined chemically.

nerves Threads of tissue that carry high-speed signals around the body.

nutrients Foods or chemicals that a plant or animal needs in order to live and grow.

omnivore An animal that eats both meat and plants. Pigs, bears, and humans are omnivores.

orbit The path taken by an object in space as it moves around another object.

ores Minerals that are important sources of metals.

organ A group of tissues that form a body part designed for a specific job. The heart is an organ.

organic matter The remains of dead plants and animals. Organic matter is an important part of soil because it contains lots of nutrients.

organism A living thing – plant or animal – that has a number of parts working together as a whole.

parasite A harmful organism that lives on or inside another plant or animal.

particle A very, very small bit of matter, such as an atom or a molecule.

repulsion The force that pulls objects apart. The same ends ("poles") of two magnets repel each other.

reservoir A place where water is collected and stored.

satellite A natural or man-made object that moves around another object. The Moon is Earth's natural satellite. Man-made satellites circle the Earth and send back information on things like weather.

species A particular kind of plant or animal such as lions or giraffes.

spore A special cell made by organisms such as fungi. Spores can grow into new organisms.

temperature The measure of how hot or cold things are.

tissue A group of cells that look and act the same. Muscle is a type of tissue.

traits The features about you that are decided by your genes.

transpiration The evaporation of water from a plant into the atmosphere.

vacuum A place where there is nothing, not even air.

vertebrae The bones that link together to form an animal's backbone or spine.

vertebrates Animals that have a backbone.

Index

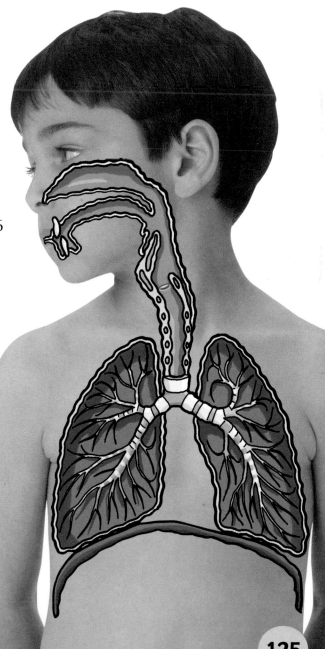

Molecule lattice

Index

Picture credits

The publisher would like to thank the following for their kind permission to reproduce their photographs:

(Key: a-above; b-below/bottom; c-centre; f-far; l-left; r-right; t-top)

Alamy Images: Arco Images 113tr; Blickwinkel 43cra, 47cl; Andrew Butterton 121bl; Scott Camazine 27cr, 95fbr, 118cb; Nigel Cattlin 23cla; croftsphoto 111tr; eye35.com 83bl; Clynt Garnham 74bl; Axel Hess 72bl; Marc Hill 107tr; D Hurst 27br; image state/alamy 21r; Images of Africa Photobank 31tl; ImageState 110bl; David Keith Jones 109tr; K-Photos 15cr; Paul Andrew Lawrence 119tl; Oleksiy Maksymenko 55tr; mediablitzimages (uk) Limited 70cr; Natural History Museum, London 17br; Ron Niebrugge 116tr; Edward Parker 114br; Andrew Paterson 68br; Pegaz 81bl; Phototake Inc 111c; RubberBall Productions 36r; Friedrich Saurer 27tl; SCPhotos/Dallas and John Heaton 47bl; Andy Selinger 43bc; Stockfolio 9bl, 59br; Adam van Bunnens 74bc; Visual & Written SL 106br; WoodyStock 106-107br; **Ardea**: Valerie Taylor 43cr; **Corbis**: Stefano Bianchetti 6cla; Car Culture 121ca; Lloyd Cluff 95cra, 102-103; Ecoscene 107tc; EPA 117tl; Martin Harvey 30-31b; Xiaoyang Liu 79cr; Michael Boys 108l; Charles E Rotkin 110cl; Paul J Sutton 13c; Pierre Vauthey 107tl; **DK Images**: Alamy/Index Stock/Terry Why 73cra, 84c; Courtesy of The Imperial War Museum, London 953719 9tl; Colin Keates 50br; Colin Keates (c) Dorling Kindersley, Courtesy of the Natural History Museum, London 61cr, 105br; Dave King/Courtesy of The Science Museum, London 56c, 56cl, 56cr; Richard Leeney 109cr; NASA 5r, 52cr, 53bl, 88r, 95tr, 99bc, 99bl, 99cr, 100tr; Rough Guides/Alex Robinson 44cb; Harry Taylor/Courtesy of the Natural History Museum, London 56tl; M I Walker 16-17; Greg Ward (c) Rough Guides 71cl; Barrie Watts 25br, 51cl; Paul Wilkinson 9c; Jerry Young 44bc; **FLPA**: Mike Amphlett 24br; Dickie Duckett 39c; Frans Lanting 46ca, 87br; D P Wilson 43crb; Martin B Withers 47r; Konrad Wothe 85br; **Getty Images**: 64470-001 111tl; AFP 74tr; Philippe Bourseiller 106tl; Bridgeman Art Library 6tc; James Burke 103tr; Laurie Campbell 47clb; Demetrio Carrasco 115tl; Georgette Douwma 14bl; Tim Flach 37tl; Jeff Foott 104-105c; Raymond Gehman 113bl; G K & Vicky Hart 91t; Thomas Mangelsen 47tl; Manzo Niikura 41tl; Joel Sartore 69c; Marco Simoni 106cl; Erik Simonsen 13tr; Philip & Karen Smith 102bl; Tyler Stableford 73crb, 89tr; Heinrich van den Berg 29ca; Frank Whitney 83r; Art Wolfe 31br; Keith Wood 110-111c; **iStockphoto.com**: Rosica Daskalova 94bl; esemelwe 74clb; Mark Evans 53cr, 61tl; Filonmar 61br; Sergey Galushko 76cr; kcline 56bl; kiankhoon 74-75c; Jason Lugo 65; Michaelangeloboy 57l; Vladimir Mucibabic 67br; Nikada 53br, 71br; nspimages 82br; Jurga R 74cla; Jan Rysavy 52b; Stephen Strathdee 21tr; Sylvanworks 69cl; **Courtesy of Lockheed Martin Aeronautics Company, Palmdale**: 80bl, 85tr; **NASA**: 87bl, 96bl, 97tl, 101cl; GSFC 94br, 96c; JPL 94bc, 95cl, 95tc, 96tr, 97bl, 100c; JPL–Caltech/S

Stolovy/Spitzer Space Telescope 95bl; MSFC 94tr; Skylab 98l; **NHPA/Photoshot**: Stephen Dalton 90br; **Photolibrary**: 115c; BananaStock 62bl; Brand X 33cla; Corbis 33tr; Paul Kay/OSF 20tr; Photodisc 56bc, 119bl; Harold Taylor 43br; **PunchStock**: Digital Vision 31t; **Science Photo Library**: 18cr, 80br, 80-81, 116-117c; Samuel Ashfield 16c; BSIP, Chassenet 83tc, 83tl; Dr Jeremy Burgess 11tl; John Durham 19tr; Bernhard Edmaier 103tl; Vaughan Fleming 95cr, 105bl; Simon Fraser 79cl; Mark Garlick 96-97ca, 97tr; Gordon Garradd 96bc; Adam Gault 17cl; Steve Gschmeissner 22tr; Health Protection Agency 81br; Gary Hincks 116bl; Edward Kinsman 69br; Ted Kinsman 7bl; Mehau Kulyk 32cr; G Brad Lewis 55br; Dr Kari Lounatmaa 49cr; David Mack 16bl; Chris Madeley 78cr; Dr P Marazzi 38tl; Andrew J Martinez 100bc, 100br; Tony McConnell 73cr, 86cr; Astrid & Hanns-Frieder Michler 14c; Mark Miller 17fcl, 17tc, 17tl; Cordelia Molloy 78bl; NASA 95br, 117c; National Cancer Institute 36l; NREL/US Department of Energy 54br; Philippe Psaila 9bc; Rosenfeld Images Ltd 67tl; Francoise Sauze 82bl; Karsten Schneider 116br; Science Source 19tl; SPL 38bl; Andrew Syred 32c; Sheila Terry 109cl; US Geological Survey 8br; Geoff Williams 75cr; Dr Mark J Winter 53cra, 59cr; **Shutterstock**: 2happy 64br; Adisa 121c; Alfgar 79br; alle 24cb, 28tl; Andresi 7cr; Apollofoto 115bl; Matt Apps 106cb; Andrey Armyagov 9cra, 58bl; Orkhan Aslanov 13tl; Lara Barrett 25br; Diego Barucco 101tr; Giovanni Benintende 5t, 96-97c; Claudio Bertoloni 7br, 81tr; Mircea Bezergheanu 118-119tl; Murat Boylu 58cb, 64crb; T Bradford 66tr; Melissa Brandes 104c; Karel Brož 14br; Buquet 37cl; Vladyslav Byelov 66bl; Michael Byrne 12b; Cheryl Casey 32cb; William Casey 4cr; cbpix 113c; Andraž Cerar 63cl; Bonita R Cheshier 60tr; Stephen Coburn 112-113cb; dani 92026 1; digitalife 4-5, 25cla, 122-123; Pichugin Dmitry 4bl, 26-27cb, 54clb, 107cr, 112-113ca; Denis Dryashkin 19cr; Neo Edmund 29crb; Alan Egginton 86cr; Stasys Eidiejus 88tl; Christopher Ewing 9cr; ExaMedia Photography 120tr; Martin Fischer 119cra; Flashon Studio 68bl; martiin fluidworkshop 82tl; Mark Gabrenya 2-3b, 22-23cb; Joe Gough 48l; Gravicapa 67tr; Julien Grondin 5c; Adam Gryko 48r, 49l; Péter Gudella 83clb; Bartosz Hadynlak 75cl; Jubal Harshaw 22br; Rose Hayes 47tc; Johann Hayman 42tr; Hannah Mariah/Barbara

Helgason 71tc; Home Studio 60br, 61bl, 127b; Chris Howey 86, 120tl; Sebastian Kaulitzki 8cr, 38c, 38cb, 39bl; Eric Isselée 28br; Tomo Jesenicnik 64clb; Jhaz Photography 73bl; Ng Soo Jiun 21bl; Gail Johnson 43tr; Kameel4u 77cb; Nancy Kennedy 27tr; Stephan Kerkhofs 44c; Tan Kian Khoon 37bl; Kmitu 40bl; Dmitry Kosterev 101cr; Tamara Kulikova 62cb, 100bl, 119bc; Liga Lauzuma 42-43; Le Loft 1911 67bl; Chris LeBoutillier 73br, 92tr; Francisco Amaral Leitão 111br; Larisa Lofitskaya 25cr; luchschen 8bl; Robyn Mackenzie 69tl; Blazej Maksym 9tc; Hougaard Malan 22-23 (background); Rob Marmion 33br; Patricia Marroquin 5clb; mashe 14cr; Marek Mnich 69tc; Juriah Mosin 41tc; Brett Mulcahy 73tl; Ted Nad 76tr; Karl Naundorf 72cr; Cees Nooij 60bl; Thomas Nord 13br; Aron Ingi Ólason 44br; oorka 120cr; Orientaly 81tl; Orla 15tr; pandapaw 28cl; Anita Patterson Peppers 73tr, 82tr; Losevsky Pavel 80t; pcross 82cb; PhotoCreate 11cl; Jelena Popic 53tr, 55tl; Glenda M Powers 30tr; Lee Prince 77cr; Nikita Rogul 54bl; rpixs 92-93cb; Sandra Rugina 115crb; sahua d 88bl; Izaokas Sapiro 78br; Kirill Savellev 106bl; Elena Schweitzer 12c; Serp 21cr, 71tr; Elisei Shafer 113br; Kanwarjit Singh Boparai7 90bl; Igor Smichkov 114cl; Carolina K Smith, M D 58cl; ultimathule 59tl; Snowleopard1 15br; Elena Solodovnikova 21br, 21cra; steamroller_blues 63br; James Steidl 8tl; teekaygee 26tl, 52-53, 87tl; Igor Terekhov 12cra; Leah-Anne Thompson 39tl; Mr TopGear 86bl; Tramper 108cb; Triff 87tr; Robert Paul van Beets 8bc; Specta 29bl; vnlit 14tr; Li Wa 8c; Linda Webb 6cra; R T Wohlstadter 117cr; Grzegorz Wolczyk 63cr; Feng Yu 86cra; Jurgen Ziewe 6br, 95crb, 98-99, 112br; **SuperStock**: age fotostock 10bl

Jacket images: *Front*: iStockphoto.com: Ivan Dinev br; Jan Kaliciak bc. *Spine*: iStockphoto.com: Serdar Yagci t

All other images © Dorling Kindersley
For further information see: www.dkimages.com

Scientists use special glass containers that can withstand high temperatures.